20.04

US AND UK
EDUCATIONAL POLICY

The Praeger Special Studies
Series in Comparative Education

General Editor: Philip G. Altbach

Published in cooperation with the
Center for Comparative Education,
State University of New York, Buffalo

US AND UK EDUCATIONAL POLICY

A Decade of Reform

Edgar Litt

Michael Parkinson

PRAEGER PUBLISHERS
Praeger Special Studies

New York • London • Sydney • Toronto

Library of Congress Cataloging in Publication Data

Litt, Edgar.
   US and UK educational policy.

   (Praeger special studies series in comparative
education)
   Bibliography: p.
   1. Education and state--United States--History.
2. Education and state--United Kingdom--History.
I. Parkinson, Michael, joint author. II. Title.
LA217.L58   379.42   78-19759
ISBN 0-03-046706-3

PRAEGER PUBLISHERS
PRAEGER SPECIAL STUDIES
383 Madison Avenue, New York, N.Y. 10017, U.S.A.

Published in the United States of America in 1979
by Praeger Publishers,
A Division of Holt, Rinehart and Winston, CBS, Inc.

9   038   987654321

© 1979 by Praeger Publishers

Printed in the United States of America

PREFACE

For several years, each of the authors has studied education policies and politics in our respective countries. Professor Litt has written numerous books and articles on American education, and Michael Parkinson is the author of The Labour Party and the Organization of Secondary Education 1918-1965 (Routledge, Kegan Paul, 1970), and other works. An invitation to present a joint paper at the 1976 International Political Science Congress (IPSC) in Edinburgh sparked this venture. Litt has been in Britain frequently, and Parkinson is familiar with American education. Not only could we contribute to each other's insights about politics in our respective native countries, but we were intrigued about common directions and problems in countries with such different political and educational structures. Convinced of a common policy agenda in Washington and London, we set out to unravel the policy context in both countries.

Our many intellectual debts require public acknowledgment. The late Stephen Wexler, staff director of the US Senate Education Committee, demonstrated enormous abilities in linking our academic and public policy concerns. Maurice Peston, then undersecretary in the British Department of Education and Science, gave generously of his time and experience to answer our questions. Arnold Heidenheimer performed the role of intellectual marriage broker by bringing us together at the 1976 International Political Science Congress in Edinburgh. Ivor Crewe of the University of Essex provided us with a keen oral critique of our IPSC paper. Nathan Glazer of the Harvard School of Education also gave us helpful insights into our work.

Two articles by Litt—"Successes and Failures of Equal Opportunity Programs in the United States," in 1974 Proceedings of the British Society for Research into Higher Education, and "British Education at the Crossroads," in Dissent (Winter 1976)—gave momentum to our collaboration. Parkinson appreciates the support of his colleagues at Washington University, St. Louis, where he is serving as a visiting professor. Litt gratefully acknowledges the support of the Connecticut Research Foundation and the National Endowment for the Humanities (NEH). The former agency has made possible typing, research, and travel support; NEH awarded him a senior fellowship (1974) that made possible his efforts to stay abreast of developments in British education policy.

It is entirely proper that a book concerned with the quality of democratic education be dedicated to our students on both sides of the Atlantic.

CONTENTS

LIST OF TABLES AND FIGURES

PART I

THE CENTRALIZATION OF POWER

1

THE POLITICS OF EDUCATIONAL REFORM

Political elites make decisions about social policies in a specific climate of opinion that determines their assumptions about what policy strategies are both possible and desirable. That climate of opinion, which has been defined as "a system of knowledge and beliefs—ideas about the causes of social problems, assumptions about how society works and notions about appropriate solutions,"[1] in turn is shaped by a variety of forces: prevailing economic conditions, the political salience of particular policies for both elites and the broader public, changing patterns of social behavior, and the analyses of social issues offered by the social science community. It is clear that during the past decade, all of these forces have been changing on both sides of the Atlantic and have contributed to a major shift in attitudes toward education and its relevance for social change. And this in turn has changed the patterns of public policy and policy making.

FROM REFORM TO RETRENCHMENT

In the 1960s, in both Britain and the United States the prevailing climate of opinion heavily emphasized the major contribution that education could make to the resolution of a number of pressing social and economic problems. Economic theory and, in particular, human-capital theory, suggested that increased educational investment and reform would increase both individual and social productivity, and hence, national economic prosperity. Social theory stressed the gains in social harmony to be derived from the creation of a more egalitarian opportunity structure in education. And in the mid-1960s the political conditions for exploiting this belief were favorable. In Britain, a strategy of educational reform was particularly attractive to the Labour Party, which throughout the 1950s had become more concerned with the status divisions in British society than with the purer eco-

3

nomic divisions of social class. In the United States the election of a president and Congress committed to social reform appeared equally auspicious for the world of education. And public demand for increased educational opportunities, and hence qualifications, to improve both social- and economic-life chances was clearly growing throughout the period.

In both countries, reformist governments took policy initiatives building upon and extending these pressures for change, trying to provide increased access to the higher echelons of the education system for those social groups who had traditionally been excluded. In Britain, greater attention was focused upon the problems of schools and pupils in deprived urban areas, as the concept of positive discrimination in favor of such pupils was tentatively developed through the educational priority-area program. There were efforts to depart from traditional subject- and examination-oriented modes of education and to make informal, child-oriented curricula more dominant in the schools. In the secondary school sector, Labour governments encouraged the growth of comprehensive education and the elimination of the system of selective schools. And in higher education, Labour presided over and financed an unprecedented period of growth in number of students, institutions, and funding.

In the United States, comparable initiatives produced, for the first time, direct federal funding of school districts targeted specifically at the economically disadvantaged; a school desegregation program that radically changed the conditions under which hundreds of thousands of children of both races were educated; and reform of the system of school financing, designed to equalize the position of poorer school districts as well as to relieve the tax burden upon property owners. At the postsecondary level, there were expanded opportunities in all parts of the sector, as well as more specific policies like affirmative-action and student-aid programs, intended to improve the educational-life chances of racial minorities and lower-income groups.

So despite the differences between the structure of their educational and political systems, both Britain and the United States moved through a period of social and economic expansion in the 1960s. On both sides of the Atlantic, the educational sphere was soon caught up in the demand for greater opportunities. Public higher education, from state universities to the community colleges, was the growth leader in America. The Robbins report of 1963 responded to comparable demand in Britain by calling for massive expansion of the university sector. By 1965, the British Labour government had launched the binary policy, designed to elevate and expand the nonuniversity sector, just as community and teachers colleges in the United States had become full-fledged postsecondary institutions. At the elementary and secondary levels, too, policy makers in Whitehall and on Capitol Hill sought to expand educational opportunity. The British comprehensive-education movement broke the monopoly of privilege held by the grammar schools. The US Elementary and Secondary Education Act, and state fiscal reform sought to break the monopoly that the suburban, white middle class enjoyed over access to college and good jobs. Even if public high school graduates comprise a significantly larger sector at Harvard, than do their counterparts at Oxbridge, the key point is that both countries were engaged in a major effort to redistribute valuable resources from the privileged to the less privileged groups in their societies.

But by the 1970s the mood of buoyant optimism that underlay these programs had dissipated, and decision makers were preoccupied with different concerns. Britain was in a period of economic doldrums, and the United States was confronting unprecedented stagflation. The reformist energies of both the American government, focusing on civil rights, and the British Labour government had been spent. Moreover, education was no longer the traditional sacred cow, even in the United States, where education had been regarded as the primary mode of assimilation and social mobility for successive waves of immigrants.

Disillusionment had set in, with the apparent failures of the educational reforms to achieve their predicted results on both the economic and social counts. In part, the problems arose from the sheer cost of the programs, especially in higher education, which were consuming a growing proportion of public expenditure, and which increasingly came into conflict with the demands of other social programs in a period of economic recession. Equally important was the failure of increased public investment in education to create the high rates of economic growth that had been aspired to and predicted in the 1960s. There was similar disillusionment with the social and educational failures of the reforms, which had not apparently materially improved either the rates of entry into the higher levels of education for working-class and minority children, or their performance within these levels. Indeed, there were growing, if broadly unsubstantiated, public fears that reform had lowered overall academic standards among children from all social classes, and growing demands for the reassertion of more traditional methods and standards to cope with the basic problems of teaching reading, writing, and arithmetic. Law and order was restored. Permissive pedagogy was out; the back-to-basics approach was in. Lavish expenditures on university buildings, research, and school facilities became suspect. These trends encouraged demands for a reevaluation of recent policies.

Social Science and Public Policy

This loss of confidence in education was exaggerated in the 1970s, as the intellectual justification for the reform programs began to disintegrate in the face of the increasingly critical assessments they experienced from the group that had constructed their original rationale, the academic social science community. One of the features of the growth of social and educational programs of the 1960s had been the direct and indirect stimulus it gave to the field of applied policy research. As A. H. Halsey and Jerome Karabel have observed, in countries that embrace welfare-state and planning ideologies, a tradition of basing institutional reform on research has always drawn academic social scientists into the policy-making process. But "it is only in the last generation that connections between government and social science have been strongly institutionalized . . . [and] caught up in a process of incorporation into the state apparatus, partly through their dependence on state funding, partly in their own right as the disciplinary bases of economic and social planning, and—most recently—partly through the emergence of a new style of administration which is potentially of immense importance: experimental public policy formation. "[2]

One major result of this process of incorporation has been the rapid growth in social-program evaluation by the academic social scientific community. As social scientists have accumulated evidence about such programs, however, the relationship between public policies and social behavior has become less, rather than more, clear. Traditional assumptions about the links between educational policies and their consequences, for example, have been challenged and often disproven, and simple solutions to social problems no longer seem appropriate. The growing social science literature has produced, ironically, "knowledge which is no better by any scientific standards, no more authoritative by any political standard, and often more mystifying by any reasonable public standard. "[3]

The Political Consequence of Increased Uncertainty

The political consequence of this new situation has been to change the climate of opinion surrounding education and to complicate the task of educational policy makers, who find themselves "constantly basing decisions on controversial and disputed research results. "[4] Although the impact of this uncertainty cannot be calculated precisely, arguably it has encouraged public decision makers to give less ideological support to expensive educational reform, especially when there is already mixed political commitment. Martin Rein describes this process generally as "policy containment," in the sense that existing programs are held at existing levels of funding, and support for more innovative programs becomes dissipated. [5] This has clearly been the experience in the United States in the past decade, and it has had relevance for Britain as well. The less dramatic, but nevertheless significant, programs implemented in Britain in the 1960s were based upon similar expectations about the positive impact that educational intervention could have upon the life chances of underprivileged children. But a decade later, many of the assumptions which underlay those programs are under serious intellectual as well as political attack. The divisions so evident within the American academy are reflected within the social science community in Britain; and the liberal environmentalist arguments that were the conventional wisdom of the 1960s are now in retreat, in the face of a conservative climate of opinion that is infinitely more skeptical about affecting radical social or economic change through education.

In a situation where severe economic difficulties have already created a mixed political commitment, politicians of both the left and the right have become willing to justify reduced support of education on the basis of such evidence. As a result, in both countries the momentum behind the reform efforts of the 1960s seems temporarily exhausted. Indeed, the policy climate has become chilled. Retrenchment, the bureaucratic way of saying that more must be done with less, has become the theme. And now policy makers in both countries face the task of dealing with rising school and university expectations with fewer monetary, cultural, and political resources at hand.

A NEW CONSENSUS: CENTRALIZATION AND LEVELING

This disillusionment with both the higher costs and the apparent failure of old policies served as an impulse for changes in public policies in both countries. And from the diverse contexts of British and American politics, a new climate of opinion emerged that incorporates two critical features. The first is a significant growth in the power of central governments to determine the direction of national education policy. In Britain the process of centralization is quite visible. The more complex American experience is characterized by an aggregation of power shifts toward the federal level. Expansionary policies, such as the Higher Education Act in the United States, and the binary policy in the United Kingdom, increased the power of government agencies. And these agencies, which had supported educational expansion during periods of prosperity, in turn became vehicles of political controls as economic conditions worsened. In the United States, increased federal aid at the school level and equalization politics at the subnational level have marked the centralization trends. In Britain the development of the pattern of nonselective comprehensive education and other

initiatives witnessed the same trends. But the government power,
which was necessarily expanded to administer the new programs, has
been used to centralize decision making and constrain the actions of
nongovernment institutions in the new period of austerity.

The second feature of this new policy climate is the emergence
of a general consensus—transcending party and institutional differences—that central power should be used to restructure educational
provision and opportunities within a cheaper, rationalized, more egalitarian framework. This trend we call policy leveling. It is a response
to the need to meet pressures for greater educational opportunities
with fewer available resources. As in Gresham's law, policy leveling
allows cheaper goods to drive out more expensive ones, leading to a
scaling down of previous expectations and, in this case, support for
the cheaper sectors of education at the expense of the more costly
ones. The pattern is crystal clear in Britain, but it markedly influences the more complicated and differentiated American system in
numerous ways. In both countries, government policy makers have
been forced to rationalize egalitarian measures in a new context of
scarcity and retrenchment. In both cases, retrenchment has been
marked by the transfer of governmental financial support to less prestigious, cheaper institutions, for ideological and economic reasons.
As a result, the university sectors, in particular, have experienced
severe financial difficulties, stemming directly from government policies in the case of Britain, and indirectly from Washington's policies,
since 1972, in the case of the United States. But in all sectors, there
has been a significant shift in resources in favor of the less well off.
In Britain the binary policy and comprehensive-education reform provided the institutional matrix for these redistributions. In the United
States the national Elementary and Secondary Education Act and the
Higher Education Act along with subnational efforts at equalization of
school finances, also moved in egalitarian directions. In Britain the
historic Labour efforts at social justice have merged with efforts to
increase efficiency and productivity, revealing elements of Fabian
antecedents. In the United States, education policy has been converted
into social welfare politics with unanticipated consequences for the
public sector.

Of course, the two systems vary in the degree of centralization
that has occurred. Localism has been a predominant force in the evolution of American education. The variety of state systems, ethnic
colleges, and racial patterns manifest a variety of cultural values un-
known elsewhere in the Western world. Yet, since World War II the
demands of national hegemony and economics have fashioned a more
centralized system, heavily influenced by research demands of government and commerce. Indeed, it is the solidification of this national
establishment that undergirds Christopher Jencks's and David Ries-

man's thesis about an academic revolution. [6] Inevitably, the weight of the federal and state governments pressed harder upon the organization and processes of American colleges and universities.

The evidence of these influences in the US system is less obvious than in centralized European systems. Perhaps 20 percent of major university budgets comes from Washington, far below the corresponding cash flow that comes from London or from Stockholm. The centralization of American national influences is cumulative; in Britain, by comparison, the power is unitary, resting with the Department of Education and Science (DES). But in Washington, there is an enormous student grant program that was fashioned by the Education Amendments of 1972. More than that, American higher education has always responded to social and governmental policies. The GI Bill, the National Defense Education Act, and the Higher Education Act—all of these resulted from pressing governmental and social needs. The advent of affirmative-action, civil-rights, and anti-sex-discrimination programs, and of the Basic Educational Opportunity Grant Program (BEOG), has provided vast enforcement power to an array of federal agencies. From the viewpoint of a specific university, this agency armada looks as formidable as the unitary Department of Education and Science does from the vantage point of a British university.

At the school level, comparable evidence of attempts at the centralization of power can be found, although with very different results in the two countries. The infinitely more simple structure of decision making in the United Kingdom has allowed the central government to successfully intervene in many policy areas from which it once stood relatively detached; and the past decade has witnessed a marked growth in the power of the DES. In the United States there have been centralizing tendencies, but they have been less overt and less obvious in their consequences. The complexities of decision making have prevented the wholly successful elaboration and implementation of a national schools policy. Nevertheless, federal funding of schools, federally imposed school desegregation, the move to reform the financing of school districts, and the diffuse movement to consolidate school districts reveal important centralizing tendencies in this most pluralistic of school systems. As Frederick Wirt has argued:

> . . . both the finance and desegregation reforms which work to foster centralization have a common feature. They represent a new shape to federalism in which policy mandates are set by national agencies but are administered locally in response to the mediating influence of a diverse society . . . [7]

The Impact: Resegregation of Higher Education

One of the most significant features of these redistributive policies is their unintended consequences; in particular, that of resegregating higher education. The architects of the 1965 Basic Educational Opportunity Grant Program in the United States, for instance, never thought that they were helping open-access institutions at the expense of better-quality students and colleges. The British Labour Party never intended that the technological institutions of the public sector should expand at the direct expense of the universities. Yet this is what occurred as the essentially expansive and progressive policies of the 1960s faced the decline in political and fiscal support for education in the following decade. The new policies of social differentiation occurred despite efforts at governmental support of the less affluent institutions and students in both countries.

It must be observed that these were not the policies of hard-hearted or antiintellectual people. After all, many of the British educational reformers were Labour Party men and women, graduates of Oxford and Cambridge. They never meant to hurt the universities in constructing the binary policy; it was simply the passage of time and the fact that their Conservative opponents agreed to do more for the technological sector. The goals were to enhance both equal opportunity, by producing more working-class graduates, and economic success, by providing the technical manpower Britain desperately needed. It was only when the power of the DES rose, and the value of the pound declined, that it dawned on them that the university sector must pay for the development of the technological sector.

This was also the case for the Civil Rights Division of the Office of Education, and other architects of key American education policies. These were liberal bastions committed to quality education. How could affirmative-action programs, student grants to the needy, and reduced direct funding to colleges and universities possibly hurt American higher education? But it was soon observed that resources are starkly finite across the sector, and not only in the medical class of the University of California at Davis. In the downward turn of the 1970s, the traditional populist view that all students and colleges are created equal soon confronted the realization that academic ability, research funds, university programs, and facilities are highly differentiated, with adverse consequences for the elite sector.

THE POLITICS OF POLICY MAKING

This book is concerned with two different nation-states that have clearly different policy-making systems. And this has implications for a comparative analysis. The British Department of Education and Science dispenses fully 60 percent of all school funds in the United Kingdom. The Department of Health, Education and Welfare provides less than 10 percent of the funds to American school districts. British universities confront none of the regional political interests that the administration of an American state university must deal with every day. Even the comparison of school reforms is skewed. School reform in America is a preoccupation, almost a crusade. Britain has rarely experienced such intensity of feeling about its schools. In Britain, one can study the local educational authority (LEA) and the actions of the central government, and not notice much of the interest-group activity that is central to the American scene. Moreover, the British plan for the comprehensive school, enacted during the last decade, resembles the plan for the American public high school, which was introduced 50 years earlier.

Equally, the inequalities in funding between British schools in different local education authorities are nothing compared to those found between the core cities and the richer suburbs of most American states. Consequently, the focus of the school reform movement in Britain was different, being an attempt to terminate a class-based, tripartite school system. In the United States the effort has been to put more funds into the hands of disadvantaged children and their schools. This is what the Elementary and Secondary Education Act, and the aftermath of <u>Serrano v. Priest</u> (1971), have been about. Put differently, the two nations are in different time periods regarding mass access to secondary and postsecondary institutions, the input of nonadministrative bodies, and even confrontation with whirlwinds of ethnic and racial sentiments.

A Common Agenda

But these differences cannot conceal the comparable policy agenda that officials in both Washington and London have come to face in recent years. The strains between demands for more equal educational opportunities and pressures to curtail costs have closed in on policy makers in both nations. The British Labour Party had fought for expanded educational opportunities through the comprehensive schools and the polytechnics. American reform took on the dimensions of a crusade on behalf of equality—affirmative action; Title I grants to aid culturally poor, deprived children; federal basic opportunity grants; and federal and state assumption of school costs historically based on unfair and burdensome local property taxes. In the 1970s all of these progressive measures have been caught in the vise of political and fiscal reaction. Granted the significant differences between the British and American systems, the impressive reality is the common dilemma faced by politicians and education policy makers on both sides of the Atlantic. Equally significant, the common policy agenda has come to be accepted by the major political parties. British Conservatives, for instance, supported the development of the poly-technics in a newly created public sector. The Nixon-Ford adminis-trations supported proposals providing open access and support for disadvantaged pupils. In both countries, more power was given to the bureaucracies: the Department of Education and Science in Britain, and the mixture of federal and state agencies that increasingly domi-nate American education policy. In their hands, retrenchment policies have become the instrument with which to rationalize costs, efficiency, and output.

Set against a broad time frame, educational opportunity in both Britain and the United States has made progress. It was not that long ago that a good college education in the United States was reserved for the sons and daughters of the wealthy. The network of private, elite prep schools led directly to the Ivy League and first-class oppor-tunities. In Britain, the eleven-plus examination set in motion the ascent to the grammar schools for the privileged few, and the descent to the secondary modern schools for the working-class masses. Few American blacks aspired to Harvard, and not many working-class families ever contemplated Bristol University, much less Oxford or Cambridge.

Much of this has changed. Our task is to assess the fruits of the policies of a decade that cultivated equal opportunity. We begin with educational policies and processes forged in the expansive decade of the 1960s. We conclude with findings drawn in the cold dawn of the restrictive 1970s. This book explores the developments in companion chapters. Chapters 2 and 3 describe the centralization of educational power in Britain and the United States. Chapters 4 and 5 assess the impact of public policies upon US and UK higher education. Chap-ters 6 and 7 discuss school reform movements in both countries and weigh their impact upon the distribution of scarce resources.

NOTES

1. David K. Cohen and Michael S. Garet, "Reforming Educa-tional Policy with Applied Social Research," Harvard Educational Review 45, no. 1 (February 1975): 21.
2. A. H. Halsey and Jerome Karabel, Power and Ideology in Education (New York: Oxford University Press, 1977), pp. 5-6.
3. Cohen and Garet, op. cit., p. 33.
4. Harvey Averch et al., How Effective is Schooling (Santa Monica: Rand Corp., 1971), p. 72.

5. Martin Rein and Sheldon H. White, "Policy Research: Belief and Doubt," Policy Analysis 3, no. 2 (Spring 1977): 239-72.

6. Christopher Jencks and David Riesman, The Academic Revolution (New York: Doubleday, 1969).

7. Frederick Wirt, "Financial and Desegregation Reform in Suburbia," in The Urbanization of the Suburbs, ed. by Louis Masoitti and Jeffrey K. Hadden (Beverly Hills: Sage Publications, 1973), p. 485.

2

THE CENTRALIZATION OF POWER
IN BRITAIN

Political relationships in British education have always been subtle, resting less on formal, legal arrangements than on complex, well-developed modes of institutional interaction. Nevertheless, if the division of authority between central government, local education authorities, and teacher associations has often been difficult to delineate precisely, it has generally been an amicable one. It is a system suffused by a set of values, most significantly by what Michael Katz has called the "long-standing and highly civilized" traditions of restraint and autonomy, which have sustained a delicate consensus among the participants about the exercise of power. Indeed, Katz has argued:

> It is the presence of these traditions rather than the formal description of authority contained in legislation that explains what at first seems a paradox: the preservation of decentralization in what is from an American (although not from a European) perspective, a centralized educational system. [1]

The traditional characterization of the system as being nationally determined but locally administered, or as being a tripartite alliance between national government, local government, and the teachers, may conceal as much as it reveals, but it nevertheless contains an essential element of truth. The system has been at once both centralized and diffuse. But, as already suggested, the economic and social changes of the past two decades have imposed strain upon that intricate set of relationships as central governments have assumed greater powers in their effort to control the impact of those developments upon the education system. One observer, for example, suggests: "While the system is apparently the most decentralized and pragmatically organized in Europe, its more obvious features cannot totally conceal a tightly knit structure based on central controls." [2]

THE CONTROL SYSTEM

The centralization of educational policy making has been most clearly characterized in recent years by the expansion of the authority and role of the Department of Education and Science. During the 1970s the DES has assumed a much more assertive role in educational policy, in relation to its partners in the educational alliance—the universities, the local authorities, and the teacher associations. Policy making, which was traditionally finely balanced between a centralized and a decentralized system, has become far less pluralistic in nature. Open, explicit policy choices have become less common, and the contributions of nongovernmental groups to decision making have been gradually restricted, as the central government has sought to impose national goals upon the rest of the system. Increasingly, this model is criticized as inappropriate for the formulation of education policy.

The model developed during the 1960s, in response to the chronic economic difficulties Britain faced and, specifically, as a result of reforms of the public expenditure-control system.[3] Inspiration for British efforts to rationalize and control public spending was derived from the earlier experience of the American government with expenditure-control systems. But their impact upon both policies and policy making in Britain was rather different than had originally been intended in the United States. There, such techniques were primarily designed to rationalize the chaotic program structure endemic to a fragmented political and bureaucratic system, and to allow more rational choices to be made from among different policy alternatives. Achieving prominence during the Great Society era, they were designed to allow policy innovation as much as to simply constrain rates of taxation and expenditure. But when introduced in Britain, with its less powerful legislature, less fragmented legislative programs, and its correspondingly more powerful central finance ministry, such techniques, rather than encouraging policy innovation, rapidly became the basis for a sophisticated system of public expenditure controls that enhanced even further the powers of the Treasury over the public purse. These powers, developed gradually, have been increasingly exercised over the public sector in the 1970s.

The system consists of a series of institutions and procedures, including the Public Expenditure Survey Committee, the Central Policy Review Staff, the Program Analysis Review, and output budgeting, which were gradually introduced from the early 1960s onward. It was designed to rationalize public expenditure by allowing ministers and civil servants the opportunity to both plan expenditure over longer five-year and ten-year periods, and carry out detailed analyses of existing and alternative government programs.

Despite reservations that may be expressed about the effectiveness of specific parts of the system, it represents a major innovation in procedure and provides Britain with one of the more effective financial-control systems available to any government. [4] Clearly, it has greatly enhanced the power of politicians and civil servants at the center to plan programs. But more significantly, it has generated a mood wherein the economic dimensions of public policies have become almost more significant than their substantive components. In an era of financial austerity, the machinery has been created that locates social policy planning almost entirely in the context of economic constraints. And the system has been used with increasing effect in the last decade by both political parties.

These changes in the broader planning machinery of the British government have been paralleled by internal changes in the Department of Education and Science, which have led to similarly increased powers. For example, the use of the highly developed system of permanent and ad hoc external advisory committees to make policy recommendations—which produced the series of expansionary reports in the 1950s and 1960s, most notably the Robbins Committee report on higher education—has been virtually abandoned in favor of internal planning. And since 1968, existing DES controls over local-authority capital planning, via the use of loans sanctioning, have been made increasingly stringent in order "not merely to promote economy and ensure minimum standards, but also to set a limit to the size of the program well into the future, to determine priority needs it will meet, and to keep a close and continuing control over each part of the process. . . ."[5]

The DES's internal planning machinery has also been strengthened. In 1966 the Labour minister of education created the first small Planning Branch, but it remained relatively weak for some years. However, the return of the Conservative government in 1970, with its greater emphasis upon business and managerial methods, led to the creation of the much more powerful Departmental Planning Organization designed to "advise the Minister on an overall coordinated education policy."[6] Collectively, these developments enabled the DES, in its own words, "to undertake a major reappraisal of educational policies,"[7] which led in turn to the publication of the critical 1972 white paper. The white paper made public, for the first time, the policy implications of the critical institutional changes that had taken place during the previous decade. And it proved to be a statement of priorities for the next decade that was of crucial importance not only for the manner in which education policy was made, but also for the future of education in Britain. The Treasury and the Central Policy Review Staff were deeply involved in this policy review, which "was dominated by the need to keep education expenditure within the new constraints that were being applied to public expenditure overall."[8] It drew to a close the era of buoyant expansion and marked the emergence of the new consensus on policy leveling and the rationalization of policy in the face of scarce resources.

The Growth of DES Control in Higher Education

Evidence of DES efforts to concentrate power in its own hands and rationalize the structure of higher education can be found in a number of different areas. Its treatment of the colleges of education since 1972 is a particularly good example. These institutions, controlled by local educational authorities, provide most of the teachers for state primary schools and the least prestigious secondary schools. Like many of their European and American counterparts, colleges of education have been traditionally underprivileged vis-à-vis the universities in terms of the qualifications of both their staffs and students, the certification they offer, the resources devoted to them, their internal government, and consequently, their public status and prestige. As a result, pressure to reform and liberalize these monotechnic institutions grew throughout the 1960s.

But the Conservative government in 1972, and the Labour government thereafter, used this demand for reform to virtually eliminate the colleges of education within the space of five years. The colleges of education had experienced the most rapid growth within the higher educational sector, throughout the 1960s, expanding student enrollment from just over 30,000 to almost 110,000 by the end of the decade. But Conservative policy outlined in the 1972 white paper, and elaborated in later departmental circulars, reversed that trend and determined that, in view of the declining birthrate and existing capacity in universities and polytechnics, the numbers of students in the colleges should be cut back to 15,000. [9] The colleges themselves were radically altered in nature by being merged into the general higher education sector. Some were merged with universities and with polytechnics. Others merged with other colleges to become new institutions offering a variety of qualifications, many of them vocational, as well as the new two-year diploma of higher education. About a dozen were permitted to remain as monotechnic teacher-training colleges, and 30 closed entirely.

This rapid closure of a large number of successful and viable colleges attracted widespread and persistent criticism of DES policy. Much of it was concerned with the arithmetical basis of the new policy, which, it was argued, seriously underestimated the need for teachers in the late 1970s and 1980s, and would lead to a significant deterioration in the staff-student ratio in the schools during those years. But most criticism was directed at the way in which the government and the DES had implemented the new policy. It was commonly argued that the DES desire to rationalize provision and cut student numbers had immediately led it to act in an arbitrary manner, which had, until the 1970s, been alien to the spirit of policy making in education. Consultation had been kept to a minimum. Decisions were taken in great haste, during the years 1972-74, when the whole structure of local government in England and Wales was already undergoing extensive reorganization, thus leaving interested parties little opportunity to press their case. [10] Nevertheless, it typified the new style of centralized decision making in education that emerged during the 1970s. As the permanent secretary of the DES observed, in giving evidence to the Committee of the Organization for Economic Cooperation and Development (OECD)—which was reviewing educational policy making in Britain—the DES believes it is possible to have participation in the process of consultation, but it is no longer possible in the process of decision making. Thus the pressures to rationalize and economize have changed traditional power relationships.

A Coordinating Institution for Higher Education

Another revealing example of the new spirit in policy making during the past five years is the DES's refusal to give a clear lead on one of the major structural problems of higher education in Britain—the absence of a central coordinating body that could control and plan the diverse parts of the higher education system. Since the beginning of the 1970s there has been a broad consensus amongst the interested parties that higher education would benefit from such an institution. Despite disagreement about the details, there has been a similar consensus that it should be a representative national body with a quasi-autonomous status similar to that recently held by the University Grants Committee (UGC). The most significant confirmation of this demand was the recommendation of the Parliamentary Select Committee on Higher Education, in 1972, that just such a higher education commission, with powers comparable to those of the UGC, should be set up to plan all of higher education. [11]

But both political parties in office have resisted the call for such an institution. It is clear that both they and the DES have been reluctant to create an equivalent of the autonomous UGC precisely because it would undermine the controls over higher education they have developed so painstakingly in the past decade. In 1972, the Conservative minister of education denied the need for a higher education commission by insisting that "we do the coordinating here."[12] A later DES statement argued that such a body would be "an undesirably centralized bureaucracy with very extensive powers."[13] By contrast, the DES has preferred to discuss the development of regional bodies to integrate and control higher education facilities, which, lacking national status and autonomy, by implication could be more easily controlled by the DES.

The University Grants Committee: Declining Autonomy

Further evidence of the growth of DES power can be drawn from its treatment of the University Grants Committee in recent years. The department has consistently attempted to change the nature and function of the UGC, both by encouraging it to exercise greater control over the internal affairs of the universities, and by increasing government control over the UGC itself. The situation has changed radically since 1969, when the UGC refused even to cooperate with the Labour government in an attempt to cut costs in the university sector. Now it is willing to engage not merely in cost-cutting exercises, but more importantly, in setting targets for the growth of particular disciplines and in the concentration of resources in selected universities and the subsequent designation of others as slow-growth institutions. Although the UGC itself has not seriously resisted this shift in the balance of power, its failure to do so has led to the criticism that it has not properly performed its traditional and unique role of sustaining the autonomy of British university education.

The UGC was established in 1919 to inquire into the financial needs of university education in the United Kingdom, and to advise the government on any grants that Parliament may consider making to the universities. In 1952, it was given the added responsibility of collecting, examining, and issuing information relating to university education throughout the United Kingdom. The UGC's historic mission has been to provide a buffer between the government and the universities by relieving the government of assuming direct financial responsibility for the universities, and by safeguarding the universities from political interference. Until 1963, the UGC was the direct concern of the Treasury, and UGC staff consisted of former Treasury civil servants. The efficacy of the UGC's buffer role between government and the universities was rooted in the loyalty of these civil servants to the UGC and in their acquired knowledge about the Treasury's political culture. Moreover, the Treasury itself was deeply committed to the buffer principle, and guarded the committee's independent status. Through 50 years of Conservative and Labour governments, the committee's autonomy was rooted in one indispensable element, namely, reciprocal confidence between the committee and the universities.

Policy relationships changed when, in 1964, responsibilities for universities were transferred from the Treasury to the new Department of Education and Science. What did not change significantly were patterns of trust among members of Britain's governing class. A 1974 University Grants Committee report affirms "that no Minister or official of the Government has ever sought to influence the sums of money paid to any individual university or to attach conditions to the grants committee."[14] What did change was fundamental policy about the allocation of educational resources within a postindustrial society. It is the responsibility of the Department of Education and Science to administer governmental policies about the distribution of resources to the university, nonuniversity, and elementary-secondary sectors of British education. When the UGC's 1974 report commented that "we are happy, in principle, to be linked with Government through a Department of Education and Science,"[15] Whitehall prose was acknowledging that the universities are now competing with the polytechnics and other sectors of education for the scarce funds available from the DES.

Traditional UGC practice accentuates "rule by the dons, for the dons." The great majority of its members are either active or retired academics. A cross section of academic disciplines and universities exists on the committee. Ad hoc working parties are created periodically to investigate new academic developments. This is professional peer review, familiar enough in American intellectual life, with two important differences. First, the UGC deals with national policy criteria in its evaluation of university developments and requirements. This requires not only frequent consultation by the UGC with the government and the universities, but also familiarity with recommendations of special commissions and educational organizations. Second, much of the UGC's work involves curriculum, program recommendations, and the core issue of university places (the number and distribution of students, and the support needed), matters that are dealt with internally in American colleges.

The major issue now facing the UGC is the growing hegemony of the Department of Education and Science as the key education decision maker. The influence of the UGC is rooted in its relations with the autonomous university sector of British higher education. The autonomy of that sector now conflicts at every turn with governmental policies, centrally administered by the DES, regarding allocation of educational resources. There has been a steady drift toward support of the public postsecondary institutions, and toward the state-maintained comprehensive schools at the expense of the universities. For example, funds for British universities were cut 5 percent (23 million uninflated pounds) during 1974, while almost an identical sum was added to the rest of the education budget. So long as the UGC could have influence at the margins—for instance, in its decision to reduce staff-student ratios in the arts subjects—then it could modify government policies dictating academic salaries, student distributions, and the amount of the quinquennium settlement. But when resource scarcity, due to Britain's economic woes, is compounded by detailed central direction, then the UGC's future is shaky. The Department of Education and Science could easily take over the administration and funding of all higher education, if government policy demands greater coordination of Britain's human and scientific resources. Replacing informal relations among the governing class with bureaucratic decision making ends any semblance of rule by the dons, for the dons.

For the present, however, despite its difficulties, the University Grants Committee functions to preserve at least limited university autonomy. Its assurances of long-term and flexible funding are assets that many hard-pressed American university presidents have cause to envy. Daniel P. Moynihan's ill-fated effort to create a National Educational Foundation offers testimony to the appeal of the UGC as a model with which to sustain university excellence. How long the UGC, and the English idea of a university it seeks to preserve, can endure will depend on future events. The tide of economic distress, Labour Party education policy, and mass social concerns are running against "peculiar institutions" created by educational elites. If this continues to be so, the University Grants Committee may disappear as a casualty of Britain's struggle for economic survival and remedial social justice.

The DES thrust for power in recent years is obvious. Indeed, it is difficult to disagree with the judgment that "the Higher Education Commission already exists, and it goes by the name of the Department of Education and Science."[16] Nevertheless, many reservations persist about the desirability of recent trends. Although it may be appropriate for the DES to accept responsibility for the planning of the educational service, given its full-time resources and technical competence, its record in the area of planning has not been reassuring. As one responsible commentator has observed:

> The long civil service tradition of self-effacement and avoidance of sensitive areas has meant that the exploration of possibilities has disappeared to vanishing point, and that the secretary's assurance that a reasonable and balanced judgement has been reached carries no conviction. [17]

The Schools and the Centralization of Power

The balance of power has also been changing in the secondary school sector in recent years as the DES has increasingly asserted its control over policy making, at the expense of both the local education authorities and the teacher associations. The traditional pattern of extensive group negotiation in policy making, with considerable discretion to vary policy left to the individual local authority, school, and teacher, has undergone great stress as the department has increasingly emphasized the national, rather than the local, character of the education service. As in the case of higher education, increased departmental intervention has stemmed from two factors: a desire to rationalize policies at a time when major economic difficulties imposed severe constraints upon the education service; and a related concern about monitoring more closely the impact of those programs which continue to be funded, in order to maximize the return on its educational investment.

Once again, a sense of disappointment with some of the reform initiatives of the mid-1960s has produced a general reaction against the liberalism of those policies, and has led the department, in particular, to focus in more detail upon the internal dynamics of educational achievement as well as upon institutional reform, to try to determine the most appropriate avenues for future developments. This has inevitably led to a growth in central power and a corresponding reduction in the power of other groups. The result of this trend has been the department's more direct involvement in a range of sensitive and critical areas of education policy from which it once remained more detached—like the curriculum, modes of public examination, inservice teacher training—as well as in the detailed financing of LEAs and the overall shape of the secondary school system.

The DES's own position on many of these issues was made most visible in the extremely controversial document on the future of the education service that it produced in 1976, the so-called Yellow Book. It was written in response to the prime minister's request for a clarification of official policy on what had increasingly come to be regarded as the critical issues facing the education service in the mid-1970s: the teaching of reading, writing, and arithmetic in primary schools; the appropriate curriculum for older children in comprehensive schools; the structure of the public examination system; and the general educational problems faced by the 16-to-19-year age groups who fail to enter higher education. The department used this opportunity to launch a searing attack on many of the most significant developments that had occurred within the nation's schools in the previous decade. It criticized the failings of child-oriented primary education; the low academic standards in secondary school, partly resulting from comprehensive-school reorganization; the failings of the teaching profession; the lack of intellectual coherence displayed in the curricula adopted by different schools and education authorities; and the alleged mediocrity of the work done by the Schools Council in the key areas of curricula and examinations in the past ten years. To remedy these deficiencies, the DES argued that greater emphasis should be placed upon academic standards and upon the creation of a universal core curriculum that would help produce greater national uniformity in academic standards. In the future, the DES argued, it should play a much greater role in these critical areas, as opposed to the LEAs and the teacher associations. To legitimate this shift in the balance of power, it recommended that the prime minister make "an authoritative pronouncement on the division of responsibility for what goes on in school, suggesting that the department should give a firmer lead."[18]

In fact, the department had been making preparations for such an assertion of power during the previous two years. In 1974, for example, it had created the Assessment of Performance Unit to encourage new approaches to the assessment of educational performance, in the hope of preparing the way for the national monitoring of standards. And it had frequently recommended expansion of the unit's activities and significance. At the same time, it had been planning a reorganization of the role of the chief inspectorate. The new system, which was revealed early in 1977, withdrew one-quarter of the inspectorate from their traditional duties as advisers and evaluators of LEAs on a regional and local basis, so that in the future they could be concentrated at the center in London, working on national surveys and studies. The aid was to concentrate the inspectorate's energies on developing national curricula and modes of assessment, and to allow them to produce results "in a form that can readily be published and disseminated,"[19] to maximize the impact of central department studies upon LEAs.

The Schools Council

But perhaps the most significant, and most politically controversial, effort by the DES to increase its power in the areas of curriculum and examinations lies in its treatment in recent years of the Schools Council. This organization had been the institutional compromise that had resulted from an earlier effort by the department to increase its powers over school curriculum and examinations in the early 1960s.[20] At that time, the teacher associations had vetoed what they regarded as the department's heretical plan to usurp their traditional powers over curriculum by creating a curriculum study group within the department. They had successfully insisted instead upon the creation of a public representative body, the Schools Council, which would determine major questions of curriculum and examinations, and which would give major weight to the views of the teachers' professional associations.

In recent years, the DES has shown a growing impatience with the work of the council, partly because of its feeling that the council had become too oriented to the needs and interests of the teaching profession, and partly because of the belief that its programs and policies had encouraged a dilution of academic standards in the schools through a preoccupation with the needs of the intellectually average child rather than with those of the gifted child. The degree of dissatisfaction, when made public in the Yellow Book, led the department into an unprecedented public confrontation with the chairman of the council, who eventually resigned. At the same time, in a very damaging decision, the minister of education rejected the council's long-awaited new proposals for the revised common examination systems, upon which it had been working for several years, and announced that she would assume responsibility herself, within the DES, for any future major changes in the examination structure.

More important, the minister announced early in 1977 that the structure of the Schools Council was to be revised, and that in the future the DES would play a much greater role in setting the goals and research agenda of the council and would significantly reduce the discretion the council had in deciding the range of topics on which it would focus. By the beginning of 1978 the new structure of the Schools Council was taking shape and it did indeed reflect the shift in the balance of power that had taken place in the recent years. The new structure called for a tripartite arrangement of committees. Lay matters would be looked after by a new body, the Convocation Committee. Professional matters would be taken care of by a teacher-dominated committee. But a third committee, Finance and Priorities, would determine the future work of the Schools Council, and it would be dominated by the DES and the LEAs, with only minority representation for the teachers. The new structure confirmed the prediction of one observer that, in view of the DES's recent rejections of the Schools Council reports, and despite the persistent criticism of the secretiveness of the DES, "what the D. E. S. now needs is a Schools Council which would carry out D. E. S. policy without the civil servants (or the politicians) seeming to have control over curriculum and exams."[21]

Control over School Finance and Structure

The central government has also exercised more detailed financial control over LEAs in recent years. In 1976, for example, in an effort to persuade LEAs to control increases in expenditure, the government reversed the trend of recent years and cut its support for local authority spending. The rate support grant for 1977-78 was reduced so that the central government's contribution amounted to only 61 percent rather than the existing 65 percent of total expenditure, and local tax rates had to be raised by 15 percent to produce existing revenue levels. At the same time that these reductions in the overall level of financial support were made, the DES has been trying to introduce an element of categorical, rather than general, aid for education so that it might have a more direct influence on the way in which the LEAs use their funds. In 1976, for example, it set apart £7 million from the budget for LEAs and allocated it specifically for teacher in-service training, which it was particularly anxious for LEAs to develop. The continuing campaign for specific grants for education to back the minister's chosen policy represents, in the view of one observer, a bid for power, by the department, "of the greatest importance to the future development of English education."[22]

These changes in conjunction with Circular 10/75, which, for the first time, specified appropriate expenditure targets for LEAs in an era of scarce economic resources, demonstrated the importance the department attached to the goal of controlling local authority expenditure; and, in the view of the Times Educational Supplement (London), they revealed "once again how precarious is the constitutional autonomy of the local government in the face of ever more determined efforts by the treasury to curb all forms of public expenditure."[23]

At the same time, the department has adopted a more interventionist posture in the future internal shape of the secondary sector, quite apart from its plans for comprehensive-school reorganization. In the future the DES will be concerned not only with the elimination of selection in secondary education, but with the particular pattern of comprehensive schools that LEAs adopt, and it will increasingly favor a single comprehensive pattern involving the creation of tertiary-level colleges serving the needs of all post-16-year-old children in the LEAs. In keeping with its concern to affect the curricula offered by the LEAs, the DES plans to conduct a survey of the work of existing comprehensive schools and of their links with patterns of social deprivation, in an effort to determine what factors internal to comprehensive schools seem to be linked with academic and social success. The implication of all these developments is that the DES believes a national, rather than a local, response is required for the task of school evaluation.

Reaction against the DES

As the DES has adopted its more assertive role in the varied fields of higher education, school curriculum, examinations, teacher training, and the patterns of expenditure and organization of schools, public criticism has mounted. The Times Educational Supplement, for example, observed that the developments marked "the reversal of the long-term trend which since the early 1920's has steadily diminished the curricula influence of the administrators and the public's representatives."[24]

One result of this continuing criticism was that the Organization for Economic Cooperation and Development, in 1975, devoted its annual analysis of national strategies for educational development entirely to the 1972 white paper and its implications for educational policy making in Britain. And that report, in a vitriolic critique of the policy-making model used by the DES, accused the DES of adopting increasingly secretive, antidemocratic decision-making procedures. The principal criticism was that the department showed a growing insensitivity to the wishes of its partners in the educational alliance, as it sought to make unilateral policy choices with minimal public discussion of their rationale or implications.

Domestic political reaction to the OECD criticisms was so intense that in 1975 the Parliamentary Expenditure Committee devoted itself to an investigation of policy making in the DES. The committee's report confirmed there was "a widespread feeling that the D. E. S. is not sufficiently open in its dealings with the various educational groups involved in education and with the public at large. "[25] It argued that the department was too secretive about the assumptions underlying its longer-term plans for the educational service and did not encourage interest groups, or indeed the wider public, to participate in discussions of long-range planning and of the overall purposes and shape of the educational service. The committee was also concerned that the DES engaged in little or no consultation with Parliament itself. To minimize these problems in the future, it recommended the creation of a new body, a Standing Education Committee—representing broad sectors of the public like the trade unions, employers, and parents—which would have "the authority and resources to contribute to strategic educational planning for the whole educational service. "[26] It was not intended to duplicate the role of existing institutions, but to provide "the education service and its clients with a second and independent view."[27] In the long term, the Schools Council would create "suitable machinery for putting the relevant issues in a longer term perspective in the light of broader social and economic trends. "[28] The Parliamentary Expenditure Committee also argued that the DES should be more willing to publish its planning documents, such as the Program Analysis Review, which underlay the 1972 white paper, to encourage the process of public debate about the future of education. And it urged the reconstruction of the Central Advisory Councils as a means of further opening up the policy-making process.

The DES, in its official reply, however, refused to accept the criticisms of the committee and simply denied that it failed to provide adequate opportunity for public consultation. It rejected the proposal for a Standing Education Commission, and ignored the Parliamentary Expenditure Committee's proposal to reconstitute the Central Advisory Councils. It did indicate that, in the future, departments would allow the publication of some departmental papers, as recommended by the committee, but not of the critical Program Analysis Review papers. Its general view, again, was that it was possible to have public participation in the process of consultation, but that it was no longer possible in the process of decision making.

DES Response: The Grand Debates

The DES attempted to deflect criticism of its growing power by initiating in 1976 a series of "grand debates" with representatives of all interested parties, designed to maximize public debate about critical future decisions in education. But despite the homage paid to the principle of consultation, the agenda for the debates confirmed that the DES had already determined the parameters of future policy. The departmental preferences were quite clear, revealing, as the Times Educational Supplement observed, "too evident a wish to simplify the 'overloaded' curriculum, and to insure a more general national pattern"; the department would play so dominant a role in future policy making that the local education authorities would be "by implication reduced to the role of local magistrates administering a national service."[29] The course of the "grand debates," and the green paper on education policy that emerged from them, did little to change that judgment or allay the fears of many in the educational world. Indeed, one Liberal Party MP argued that the DES had concealed its real purposes throughout, and had "set up the current grand debate to draw up support for its views on education standards." He called, with no success, for a Parliamentary Select Committee on Education "to ensure that educational policy making is subject to public examination."[30]

The primary concern of the green paper that emerged from the grand debates of 1977 was, predictably, the curriculum. The government intent was to establish a "core" or "protected" part of the curriculum, which would be applied on a national basis and thus limit local diversity. Although relatively little detail was made available, many observers agreed the report demonstrated that the government was going to become deeply involved in areas which, for 50 years, had been regarded as being outside its sphere of influence. It was, in the words of the Times Educational Supplement, a "turning point in educational history," in the sense that "something—the role of the D. E. S. — will never be quite the same again."[31]

A circular on curriculum review, released later in 1977, required LEAs to collect and report data in order to coordinate local policies in a wide number of curricular issues. The minister denied this was an attempt to "hijack" the curriculum, but rather, a fact-finding mission, so that the central government could play its legitimate part and ensure that national needs were being met. The major teachers' spokesmen, the National Union of Teachers, disagreed, however, and advised individual teachers and representatives on committees to refuse to cooperate with the survey, which they regarded as the thin end of the wedge of centralized control. The enterprise was, in its view, "a serious departure from a curriculum devoted to schools who can best take account of local needs."[32] The debate over the centralization of the curriculum continues, but the general trends are clear and reflect the expansion of DES power so evident in other areas. In one stern judgment, they reflect "the collapse of local authority influence in educational policy-making."[33]

CONCLUSION

The last decade has witnessed a secular growth in the power of central government at the expense of other groups in the educational subgovernment. The need for economy, combined with a wish to achieve specific social goals, has led to greater governmental efforts to impose national goals on the educational system, in place of those advocated by either producers or consumers of education, at national or local levels. In fact, of course, the central government had always played a major role in the organization and provision of education in Britain, especially in the school sector. But the cases of higher education and of curriculum are different. Far more discretion was allowed to those responsible for providing the service, and the new policies in these areas represent a significant break with tradition. At what point the process might end, and costs of centralization of authority outweigh the benefits, remains to be seen.

NOTES

1. Michael Katz, Introduction, in Maurice Kogan, The Government of Education (New York: Citation Press, 1971), p. 7.

2. Anne Corbett, "Education in England and Wales," in Education in Great Britain, edited by Robert Bell et al. (London: Routledge, Kegan Paul, 1974), p. 2.

3. For an excellent discussion of these issues, see Howard Glennester, Social Service Budgets and Social Policy (London: Allen & Unwin, 1975).

4. See Hugh Helco and Aaron Wildavsky, The Private Government of Public Money (London: Macmillan, 1974).

5. Glennester, op. cit., p. 143.

6. Times Higher Educational Supplement (London), July 27, 1972.

7. Organization for Economic Cooperation and Development, Educational Development Strategies in England and Wales (Paris: OECD, 1975).

8. Glennester, op. cit. , p. 148.

9. OECD, op. cit.

10. See J. S. Lukes, "Government Policy over Higher Education," Aspects of Education, no. 18, March 1975.

11. Parliamentary Expenditure Committee, Future of Higher Education, vol. 1 (London: Her Majesty's Stationery Office, 1972).

12. Times Higher Educational Supplement, December 8, 1972.

13. Times Higher Educational Supplement, June 6, 1973.

14. University Grants Committee, Annual Report (London: Her Majesty's Stationery Office, 1974), p. 35.

15. Ibid.

16. Times Higher Educational Supplement, April 6, 1973.

17. P. Armitage, "Planning in Practice," in Decision-Making in British Education, ed. Gerald Fowler et al. (London: Heinemann, 1973), p. 226.

18. Times Educational Supplement, October 15, 1976.

19. Times Educational Supplement, February 4, 1977.

20. See R. A. Manzer, Teachers and Politics (Manchester: Manchester University Press, 1970).

21. Times Educational Supplement, June 17, 1977.

22. Times Educational Supplement, May 27, 1977.

23. Times Educational Supplement, November 19, 1976.

24. Times Educational Supplement, October 15, 1976.

25. Parliamentary Expenditure Committee (H. C. 621), "Policy Making in the Department of Education and Science," mimeographed (London, 1976), para. 75.

26. Ibid. , para. 93.

27. Ibid.

28. Ibid. , para. 95.

29. Times Educational Supplement, February 11, 1977.

30. Times Educational Supplement, March 11, 1977.

31. Times Educational Supplement, July 22, 1977.

32. Times Educational Supplement, December 2, 1977.

33. Times Educational Supplement, March 11, 1977.

3

THE CENTRALIZATION OF POWER
IN AMERICA:
THE CASE OF HIGHER EDUCATION

Compared with Western Europe, including Britain, power is highly diffused within the American higher education sector. The historical emphasis upon state and local initiatives, the influence of private foundations and institutions, and the dispersion of responsibility within the national government present a distinctly pluralistic pattern. Clearly, the American context is hostile to those who seek to fashion a coherent, Europeanized national education policy. Commenting on his efforts to secure a National Higher Education Foundation in the Nixon administration, Daniel P. Moynihan expresses these frustrations:

> Had we thought that categorical aid distorted the relations of the higher education community to the Federal government before the program was announced, we were utterly convinced of the fact in the aftermath. Corrupted would not be too strong a term. No one seemed able to think of the whole subject. Few, even, seemed able to think of the interests of a single, whole institution. A major presidential initiative which, right or wrong, was at the very least the product of some thought and analysis was greeted by silence on the part of precisely those institutions that are presumably devoted to thought and analysis. [1]

Even a greatly increased level of central government expenditures in the United States is unlikely to fundamentally shape policy outcomes, given the multiplicity of key actors at both the national and subnational levels. The point is strengthened by comparative studies of educational policy making:

> The financial leverage that the central government exerts is only one component of the instruments that are neces-

sary to implement educational reform. There is little in
the American experience to suggest that an increase in
the federal financial contribution to educational expenditure to, say 30%, would have a corresponding increase in
the equalization of opportunity. In education the variety of
possible relationships between political parties, bureaucracies, professional groups and the clients make it especially difficult to expect meaningful structural reforms
to result merely from budgetary reallocations. What successful reforms seem to require are not merely a responsive public opinion but good links between the party and the
bureaucracy, and within the bureaucracy itself, which can
sustain the reform initiatives generated by central government funds. [2]

Nevertheless, there has been profound centralization in recent
years in American higher education as the federal role has grown
markedly. Between 1955 and 1978, all public spending for higher education grew from $2 billion to $16 billion; the proportion of college
students attending public institutions grew from one-half to three-
fourths of the total number of postsecondary students; the number of
students attending postsecondary institutions doubled; and the amount
of federal government support doubled. The implication of these developments has been a growing pattern of control exerted by Washington over the character of colleges and universities. One participant
in national educational politics expressed the enormity of this influence in this fashion:

> Part of my learning has been the scope and essentiality
> of the edifices, privileges, and encouragements presently
> made available to institutions of post-secondary education
> by the government. . . . The protections and dispensations
> range all the way from tax exemptions and direct appropria-
> tions to student loans, risk guarantees, contract enforce-
> ment, campus security, fair personnel practices, support
> for basic and applied research—where does one begin or
> end? [3]

In truth, Washington responds to pressing social problems—
scientific advancement in the 1950s, civil rights in the 1960s, vocational training in the 1970s—under the rubric of educational programs.
Consequently, the cumulative impact of federal action exists despite
the absence of a coherent, stated national policy. Joel Spring caught
the essence of this reality when he observed that it

has been directed toward the creation of a rationalized and controlled labor market through the sorting function of the public schools and the control of social conflict arising from racial discrimination and inequalities in the distribution of income. Ideally the schools were to provide distribution of human resources to meet the needs of an increasingly stratified and organized economic system. This has been the goal of national programs such as Selective Service, the National Defense Education Act, parts of the war on poverty, and career education. In terms of controlling social conflict, the war on poverty was an attempt to institutionalize social conflict caused by the pursuit of upward social and economic mobility. Belief in the power of the school to provide economic mobility was to replace the bitterness caused by discrimination and inequalities in the social system. Disruptions in the social system caused by the pursuit of social advancement were to be curved by focusing the American dream of opportunity within the walls of the schoolhouse and rationalizing it in competition for grades, test scores, and diplomas. [4]

The point is that federal policies are instruments of both social welfare and social control. The mix is influenced by the policy context, so that a transition from a growth to a retrenchment period in education manifests important changes in policy directions. It is in this sense, the accelerating control over educational institutions, that we speak of greater centralization within the American system.

THE GROWTH OF THE FEDERAL ROLE

The growth in central government power resulted from the rapid growth of federal support for higher education during the 1950s and 1960s; and from a related broadening of the goals of federal policy—from a narrow concern with the needs of the national economy, and especially demands for manpower, to broader social goals, such as the support of a more balanced system of higher education, providing greater equality of access to a more broadly based clientele.

Prior to 1958, and the National Defense Education Act, the federal commitment to higher education was a modest one. A decade later, it had grown to include grants for undergraduates, federal direct and guaranteed loans, work-study programs and graduate fellowships, aid for construction, and a range of other categorical programs. For ten years after 1958, the growth in federal aid programs almost matched the growth in the higher education sector itself. And the sec-

tor prospered. During the decade of the 1960s, for example, it has
been estimated that student enrollments doubled, income and expenditures tripled, and expenditure for construction quadrupled. Foundation support for education at all levels increased 500 percent in the
ten years between 1955 and 1965. During the same period alumni business and nonalumni support for colleges more than doubled.[5]

The Post-1968 Recession

However, the secular trends of the 1960s did not continue, and
at the end of the decade many institutions were struggling with the financial consequences of their too-rapid expansion. The economic conditions of the 1970s present a marked contrast to those of the 1960s.
Whereas growth in enrollment doubled during the 1960s, by the 1980s,
it is estimated the growth rate will reach zero. In the 1960s, faculty
increased by 27,500 annually; by the 1980s, it is predicted there will
be no growth in the number of faculty. Opportunities for promotion
have declined. In the 1960s, less than 50 percent of faculty had tenure;
in the 1970s, it had reached 66 percent. Between 1960 and 1972 the
percentage of the gross national product spent on higher education,
excluding capital construction, rose from 1.1 percent to 2.2 percent.
By 1975, it had fallen back to 2.1 percent. Federal research funds
rose at 8 percent a year throughout the 1960s. By the mid-1970s, they
were static in constant dollars. During the 1960s, new colleges were
added at the rate of one per week. During the 1970s, colleges failed,
merged, or changed from private to public status. By the 1970s, federal outlays for construction were cut by 90 percent from their peak;
state and private sources of construction funds correspondingly decreased.[6] In the late 1960s, higher education was forced to seek alternative forms of financial security. The federal government became that guarantor after 1972.

Growing Federal Intrusion

These recent changes have important implications for relationships between government and higher education. During the initial
phase of support for higher education, after World War II, the federal
government was primarily concerned with the return on its investment, in terms of the production of new knowledge, technologies, and
specialized manpower. It intervened relatively little in the internal
affairs of the universities it sponsored. But changes in the direction
of policy since the mid-1960s, and, in particular, the specification
of broader federal goals for the system of higher education, have increasingly involved the federal government as well as state governments in the internal life of institutions they help finance.

The central issue raised by these developments is the future role of the federal government in higher education, in a period of great financial uncertainty. The goals the federal government sets, and the ways it seeks to implement them, now have enormous significance for the world of higher education. A number of important issues related to these goals have to be resolved, including the nature and level of financial support the federal government will offer widely differing kinds of institutions in higher education; the proper limits that can be placed upon government intervention in the internal affairs of higher education, so that a balance may be struck between institutional autonomy and public accountability; and the reconciliation of the frequent conflict between demands for the pursuit of social justice and the needs of inherently elite institutions. In the recent past, many of those issues, although obviously present, did not have to be confronted, since the easy availability of funds meant that serious choices between competing priorities often could be avoided. Institutions of higher education could try to achieve all their goals simultaneously. The new steady state conditions have radically altered that situation. Future federal policies will have major implications in the new situation.

As Martin Trow has observed, governmental intervention would inevitably have grown as the postsecondary education sector grew in size, social impact, and cost. But it has been further increased by the fact that growth has occurred in the nonelite public part of the postsecondary sector, where governments are more anxious and more able to further clarify the goals of the institutions, and where "state agencies, not universities, play the decisive role."[7]

One major result, Trow has argued, has been increased planning, and the growth in the power of administrators, both on campus and in government agencies, to make decisions about higher education. During the expansionary period, administrators generally attended less to the academic questions of mission and programs, and more to managerial questions of budget and effective management. But nonexpansionary conditions have forced critical educational decisions to be made by the administrators. This has created strain since administrative decisions about the virtue and viability of institutional practices are based on a different set of criteria than that which academics might employ. The problem is worsened when the administrators are not from the university itself, but are "located in the administrative departments of government."[8]

In the new situation, maintaining the distinction between the public and private lives of higher education has become very difficult. Decisions about the public life of the system—its size, cost, and government—have traditionally been made by politicians and administrators. But increasingly these decisions impinge, with very unpredictable effects, upon the private life of the institution, that is, the activities of faculty and students in both teaching and research. This has generated tensions and strains for institutions and decision makers, and constitutes, in Trow's terms, a "serious threat to the freedom and autonomy of public higher education."[9]

Some empirical support for this argument may be found in Earl Cheit's analysis of the response of a variety of institutions to the changed financial conditions they faced in the 1970s;[10] the study revealed how all of them had significantly centralized their administrative practices, and were on route to becoming "managed institutions," in the sense that "the administrator is now becoming the key element in deciding whether, when, and in what terms change is possible."[11] Financial austerity had drawn administrators from the periphery to the center of higher education policy, and it is "around their calculations that increasingly others must revolve."[12]

Similar trends were identified by the Carnegie Foundation's analysis of developments in over 1,200 colleges and universities, which found an intensified struggle for authority within institutions, an increase in the ratio of students to staff, and a decline in the quality of programs, students, and, to some extent, faculty.[13] Conflicts over authority within institutions had led to the decision-making power being shifted progressively upward in the administrative hierarchy—at first, from the department to the campus administrator; then from the campus to a system board; and finally, from a system board to a coordinating agency. This pattern in the shift of authority was found in both public and private institutions, in national research-oriented universities as well as junior colleges.

In part, an increased concern for the efficient use of resources in higher education, with greater emphasis placed upon centralized planning, was probably necessary and desirable in view of the diffuse patterns of growth in the 1960s. But the problem remains, at what point do the efforts of the federal government and state government's to achieve their goals begin to have a detrimental effect upon the primary goals of higher education?

Affirmative Action and Equality of Opportunity

The most visible and controversial example of the federal government's recent growing involvement in higher education is its affirmative-action program, which since the early 1970s has tried to redress discrimination against ethnic minorities and women in higher education. The policy has raised a number of difficult issues of philosophy and practice as the government has tried to exercise pressure on universities to change aspects of their recruiting, promotion, remuneration, and education policies to eliminate discrimination. These problems have stemmed from a number of sources, including the general difficulty of specifying the principle of affirmative action in an academic context; the administrative burdens and costs the policy has imposed upon the institutions involved; and the conduct of the various federal agencies involved in administering the program.

An overview of US affirmative-action policy is clearly set forth by Nathan Glazer:

> A new course in dealing with the issues of equality that arise in the American multiethnic society has been set since the early 1970's. It is demonstrated that there is discrimination or at least some condition of inequality through the comparison of statistical patterns, and then racial and ethnic quotas and statistical requirements for employment and school assignment are imposed. This course is not demanded by legislation—indeed by any reasonable interpretation of the Constitution. Nor is it justified, I have argued, by any presumed failure of the policies of nondiscrimination and of affirmative action that prevailed until the early 1970's. . . . But in the early 1970's, affirmative action came to mean . . . the settling of statistical requirements based on race, color, and national origin for employers and educational institutions. [14]

The expansion of governmental control over colleges and universities began with the profound changes described in the intent of the 1964 Civil Rights Act, which committed the federal government to the diminishing or rectifying of discriminatory hiring practices in firms and in institutions having or seeking contracts with the federal government. [15] The bureaucratization of governmental civil rights policy began with this directive:

> An affirmative action program is a set of specific and result-oriented procedures to which a contractor commits himself to apply every good effort. The objective of these procedures plus such efforts is equal employment opportunity. Procedures without effort, undirected by specific and meaningful procedures, is inadequate. An acceptable affirmative action program much include an analysis of areas within which the contractor is deficient in the utilization of minority groups and women. [16]

The path was clear to routinize the civil rights mandates and transform them to serve internal agency goals. An enforcing agency could compile a winning record more readily through specific case-

by-case minority-group employment than by achieving the more difficult task of increasing the flow of qualified minority talent into the
labor market. This involves a fundamental shift from the goal of anti-
discriminatory equal opportunity to preferential treatment for designated minorities. In the aftermath of the 1964 Civil Rights Act, President Johnson used affirmative action in a rhetorical sense—the clear
intent was to prevent discrimination:

> The contractor will not discriminate against any employee
> or applicant because of race, color, religion, sex, or na-
> tional origin. The contractor will take affirmative action
> to ensure that employees are treated during their employ-
> ment without regard to their race, color, religion, sex,
> or national origin. [17]

However, by 1969, the Labor Department shifted the goal to the
full utilization of minority labor. The underutilization of minority
workers is itself a presumption of discrimination. Consequently, "goals
and timetables must be developed by the contractor to correct these
deficiencies and, thus, to increase materially the utilization of minorities and women at all levels and in all segments of his work force
where deficiencies exist."[18] By 1971, the Department of Health, Education and Welfare's Civil Rights Division mandated preferential
treatment of minorities to fulfill the affirmative-action policy:

> Affirmative action has developed a wonderful Catch-22
> type of existence. The employer is required . . . to
> state numerical goals and dates when he will reach them.
> There is no presumption of discrimination. However, if
> he does not reach these goals, the question will come up
> as to whether he has made a 'good faith' effort to reach
> them. The test of a good faith effort has not been spelled
> out. From the employer's point of view, the simplest way
> of behaving to avoid the severe penalties . . . is simply
> to meet the goals. . . . It is hardly worth trying to catch
> the agencies in this transparent ploy: The evidence is over-
> whelming, as 'affirmative action' plans are turned back
> under threat of cancelled contracts and legal procedures.[19]

Enforcement of Affirmative Action

Enforcement of the various antidiscrimination regulations began in earnest after 1970. In the spring of 1970, Harvard was the first
private institution, and Michigan the first public institution, to be in-
vestigated by HEW as a result of complaints of sexual discrimination

lodged against them. By 1973, complaints on these grounds had been brought against 500 of the 2,500 major institutions of higher education. Between January 1970 and January 1974, 20 universities had a temporary block placed on new contracts or renewals worth $28.5 million, because they failed to meet affirmative-action compliance regulations, either by failing to supply the relevant data or, for example, failing to submit acceptable affirmative-action plans. In June 1975, the Civil Rights Division created great controversy by threatening to withhold approval for contracts totaling $65 million and involving 29 major universities, unless they produced acceptable affirmative-action plans or subscribed to one drawn up by the Civil Rights Division itself, within 30 days. Compromises were eventually arranged, but government-university relationships have remained strained ever since.

The equal-employment thrust of the 1964 Civil Rights Act was directed against trade unions and industrial firms. Subsequent application to colleges and universities fundamentally changed the concept of labor economics. While an industrial firm conforms to the model of a centralized hiring hall, the labor practices of American universities are a decentralized composite of departmental, market, and professional factors. De facto hiring is done in specialized subjects within disciplines, rather than within the university as a collectivity. Consequently, enforcing the application of statistical goals for minority hiring was unrealistic at the outset—a problem compounded by both the tenure system and the downturn in available positions in the 1970s. Affirmative-action procedures could work, at least partially, in growth periods; they were converted into a zero-sum game, by which a white male might be replaced by a minority employee, in retrenchment periods. Indeed, one of the principal ironies of the program is the timing of its introduction. During the rapid expansion of the 1960s, for example, the number of faculty in higher education doubled, and 30,000 new faculty were recruited annually. At that time, increased representation of women and ethnic minorities, if aggressively pursued, could have been at least partially achieved. But during the 1970s, the reduction in expansion produced a rapid drop in the demand for new faculty. And in the 1980s, it is anticipated the figure may drop to 6,000, almost wholly devoted to the replacement of existing staff. In this situation, federal attempts to increase female and minority representation are clearly going to distort the market even more and produce even greater inequities of treatment.

The growth of affirmative-action enforcement also saw an expansion of the enforcing agencies. Between 1972 and 1975, the number of investigators on the staffs of the Civil Rights Division and the Equal Employment Opportunity Commission (EEOC) increased from 60 to 285. Indeed, these two agencies' budgets increased significantly under the Nixon-Ford administrations, in contrast to the fate of most other social programs. The Department of Labor, the Civil Rights Division of the Health, Education and Welfare Department, and the EEOC, created by the 1964 Civil Rights Act, all had a hand in the process. Staff members tended to be representatives of aggrieved minorities, but hostile to the idea of an autonomous university. A student of Washington affirmative-action enforcement offers this observation:

> The staff of these agencies is selected in tight conformity to an ideology that distrusts universities and colleges. Of course, these people are in favor of feminist and black goals, but more importantly they were at Berkeley or at Harvard in the late 1960's and as veterans of the anti-war and civil rights movements, they simply will not forgive those institutions for getting rid of the young, radical professors with whom they closely identified. The commitment and mentality of the staffs cannot be understood without knowing about their own campus experiences during that turbulent period. [20]

Criticisms of federal agency administration of the program are rife. The judgment of the Carnegie Council, for instance, was that "seldom has such a good cause spawned such a badly developed series of federal mechanisms."[21] The criticisms made by universities and recounted by the council were legion: too many contradictory guidelines and regulations rarely compatible with the relevant features of higher education; too many agencies competing to enforce the program; too-long delays in processing plans and complaints; too-little predictability about the behavior of the HEW regional offices administering the program; and too many remedies, carried out through too many channels, preventing reasonably rapid resolution of cases.

Many of the criticisms stemmed from the lack of quality, and of familiarity with higher education, among federal agency staffs. But a more intractable problem was the missionary zeal of many of the agencies, which led them to adopt an antielitist posture; for example, the selection in June 1975, for the most intensive scrutiny, of the most prestigious of the 1,000 institutions that were subject to affirmative-action requirements. The Carnegie Council's judgment was that inept administration of the program had created a backlash of resentment against the federal government, which was separate from the backlash against the principle of affirmative action per se.

Nor was the expansion of governmental power confined to the executive branch. The Congress also bears substantial responsibility for the expansion of power and control:

In 1972, where there was already opposition on the part
of business, labor, and the academic community to the
emerging pattern of hard affirmative action, Congress
voted additional powers to the Equal Employment Opportunity Commission. Congress well knew these powers
would be used to follow up immediately on the EEOC's
victory over the largest private employer in the country,
and with pressures against states and cities everywhere
to follow patterns of proportional representation in employment. Clearly, Congress could have . . . accepted
the point of view of such major constituencies as business, labor, the universities, and city and state governments, most of whom would have been happy to have been
relieved of the burden of recordkeeping, test changing,
defense litigation, and the like that Congress was impos-
ing on it. [22]

By 1976, affirmative-action policy was modified to increase,
from $1 million to $10 million, the contract level at which federal
agencies must conduct prereview audits for affirmative-action compliance. The level at which a federal contract holder is required to
develop a written affirmative-action plan for promoting and hiring
women and members of minorities was changed from a firm employ-
ing at least 50 persons and holding a federal contract of at least
$50,000, to a firm employing at least 100 persons and holding a fed-
eral contract of at least $100,000. Moreover, the onerous practice
of suspending or denying a federal contract, when a complaint was
filed, was altered so that an institution had to be granted a formal
hearing before enforcement could be brought to bear.

Nothing in these proposals changed the fundamental use of statistical goals and timetables or the concept of proportionate hiring as
the basis of affirmative-action policy. Nor did they change the reality
that the process of governmental control proceeded independent of—
and, in many cases, contrary to—the actual progress made in employ-
ing women and minorities. Thomas Sewell finds that academic salaries
in 1969-70 for black academics with a Ph. D. averaged exactly $62 a
year below those of white academics with a Ph. D. [23] The average
1968-69 academic-year salaries of full-time female academics who
were never married—and it is marriage that is the critical factor in
curtailing female careers—were slightly higher than those of males
who were never married, and single academic women with a Ph. D.
achieve the rank of full professor more often than do other academics
with similar years of experience. Regarding the charge that women
and minorities are frozen out of the recruitment pattern by an "old-
boy network," Sewell finds that both women and blacks receive their

Ph. D. s at the top universities (the old-boy network) a higher percent-age of the time than do white men. Indeed, a case can be made for the proposition that affirmative-action pressures aid those minority members who least need it:

> Actually it is the most qualified blacks (measured by qual-ity of doctoral-granting institutions and by publication rec-ord) who have the greatest edge over their white counter-parts, while the least qualified blacks do not earn as much as the least qualified whites. . . . Black academics who have published five or more scholarly articles average about $3,000 per year more than white academics who have published five or more scholarly articles, while black fac-ulty who have published nothing earn slightly less than white faculty who have published nothing. Insofar as this is at-tributable to "affirmative action" pressures, it suggests that the program has its greatest financial impact on those blacks who needed it least. [24]

The pitfalls in using gross categories of race and sex is further illustrated by Sewell. Orientals tend to cluster in the higher-paid natural sciences, but productive Oriental scientists receive signifi-cantly less pay than equally productive whites and blacks. In top uni-versities, some women who have never married earn slightly more than men who have never married, when both groups have published. In unranked institutions, unmarried women without publications earn 45 percent more than men who have neither married nor published. The preference of qualified women for teaching, and the choosing of marriage, or a particular field, and other preferences (for example, the finding that black faculty concentrated in black colleges would not move for less than a $6,000 yearly increase) undermine the rigidity of statistical hiring. Not only did black income rise at a higher rate than white income in the 1960s—before affirmative action—but the same period saw a marked increase in marriage and childbearing among educated women—factors which depress career prospects. So the affirmative-action program accomplished little in raising the gross salaries of preferential minorities, and most benefited the highly qualified women and blacks within the academic labor pool. Yet, the costs might have been worth even these effects were it not for other factors:

> If the affirmative action program were merely inane, fu-tile, and costly, it might deserve no more attention than other governmental programs of that description. But it has side effects which are negative in the short run and

perhaps poisonous in the long run. While doing little or nothing to advance the position of minorities and females, it creates the impression that the hard-won achievements of these groups are conferred benefits. Especially in the case of blacks, this means perpetuating racism instead of allowing it to die a natural death or fall before the march of millions of people advancing on all economic fronts in the wake of "equal opportunity" laws and changing public opinion. [25]

The major beneficiaries of affirmative-action policies have been federal bureaucracies and professionals hired to administer the morass of rules, procedures, and plans that affect every college and university in the land.

Frustrated Control

The fact that America lacks a classic centralized educational policy does not mean that there is an absence of centralized control. Indeed, the case of affirmative action shows that frustrated efforts to implement new policies often increase the amount of red tape, paperwork, and other symptoms of bureaucratic maladies. Were affirmative action the only example of Washington's effort to force democratization in colleges and universities, then the threat to educational autonomy would be less severe. On the contrary, the statistical approach to the hiring of women and minorities is duplicated in numerous efforts to force choice by authoritative and repetitive administrative means.

In 1972, Washington launched the Basic Educational Opportunity Grant Program and related student aid programs designed to upgrade access to postsecondary education. The consequences of these efforts are detailed elsewhere. The point we wish to make here is that the ideas of student choice and equal opportunity themselves greatly enhanced the power of federal and state bureaucracies. The evolution of student aid programs did little to enhance the autonomy of American education. Not only did the funding limits channel unselective students into unselective institutions, but the net funding distribution actually reduced bloc grants directly available to colleges and universities. Consequently, retrenchment merely aggravated social problems without providing new remedies. What was provided were enhanced powers for federal and state bureaucracies in awarding, monitoring, and administering student aid programs. Lacking control over the diffuse American education system, Washington could only exert limited control over the quality of education to be received by the new beneficiaries of federal largesse. The result was frustration, leading to endless efforts to alter the form of the student aid practice. By 1976, the Con-

gress proposed to raise the BEOG maximum grant from $1,400 to
$1,800. However, it could do little about the rising costs of college
tuition, the quality of education received by BEOG recipients, or the
fact that BEOG students were priced out of expensive universities.
Moreover, the Congress agreed to provide institutional funding for
continuing education, academic facilities, and community colleges—
three programs that had been reduced in the allocation of resources
since 1965. The catch was that these programs would be funded at the
rate of one institutional dollar for each student aid dollar, above a
$2.8 billion student aid ceiling. A critic responded that the Congress
"didn't tackle the basic problems of higher education: the funding of
public versus private sectors and student access to the colleges of
their choice. And they've also made certain that the funding for education won't be raised as an issue in the Congress for another four
years."[26]

Caught in the spirit of equal-access education, Washington
merely tinkered with a student funding mechanism that avoided the key
problems of centralized support for a nation's educational system.
However, the mushrooming of student aid programs since 1965 has
greatly enlarged the federal and state bureaucracies—for example,
the moribund Office of Education—directly charged with the administration of the expanded student aid program. The pattern is also ob-
servable in career-education efforts. Beginning in 1971, a concerted
effort was made to directly relate the world of education to the world
of work. Secretaries of Health, Education and Welfare joined congressional leaders and outside critics in complaining that the United States
lacked an effective career- and vocational-education program. They
rejected the assumption that "more higher education is better without
asking how universities could provide civilizing experiences of intrinsic value, and how the expanding, but distinct, demand for vocational
and technical training could also be met."[27]

In 1972, a fund for the improvement of postsecondary education,
new vocational aid measures, and innovative career-education programs were established by the federal government. Now these programs could hardly be expected to succeed unless the political economy provided available jobs for trained manpower. Of course, this
problem is not the fault of governmental planners in education and
manpower training. Their problem is much more fundamental, namely,
that there is no coherent national policy that supports these objectives.
The Swedish system can regulate the availability of university and
technical education, to match the changing nature of the Swedish economy. The British could embark upon a binary policy that reallocates
scarce resources from the university to the polytechnic and vocational
side of the higher education system. But the American system is decentralized in terms of institutional control, and regulated by programs

such as student aid and affirmative action. Consequently, the pattern of multiple programs being initiated in career education resembles the basic direction of centralized power in the American national system.

Bureaucrats can offer carrots and sticks—in career education, affirmative action, student aid—to enhance the success of their program. What they cannot do is influence the success of the policies that underlie their efforts. Affirmative-action agencies cannot increase the hiring of minorities in a tight market; career educationalists cannot plan programs that conform to the distinct needs of private industry and the government itself; and the Office of Education cannot use academic ability as a criterion in awarding federal student aid money. At the end of the day, this produces more frustration and bureaucratic maladies than occur in Europe, where ministers can set forth and execute clearly derived policies. The tendency to create programs that meet constituency needs, without control of policy structures that affect the success of policy outcomes, increases the frustration of efforts at centralization of American higher education. This factor—rather than the sheer control of expenditures—most distinguishes the pluralistic American system. And it is the cumulative nature of power centers that ultimately buries American educational institutions under a sea of regulation, conformity, and detail that impedes the execution of educational functions.

Ameliorative Measures

In this situation, the key need is to reform the nature of federal control. Direct aid to colleges and universities is required, even at the expense of student aid and other programs. Moynihan's efforts toward a National Foundation for Higher Education deserve to be revived. Whatever the form, broad grant support would provide colleges and universities with the resources to deal with internal demands, including the demands for equal opportunity. It is unfortunate that at the moment of budget cutbacks, there is little federal support that can be used in a flexible way.

What are the criteria for allocating direct federal aid to colleges and universities? Considering the evidence, it is clear that all efforts to undermine or ignore qualitative standards have failed as social, economic, or political measures. It is ironic that reliance upon standards, the last refuge of conservative academics, turns out to be the best way of preserving the progressive idea that higher education is open to all who merit it, regardless of race, sex, religion, or nationality.

First, some educational criterion of student selectivity (for example, SAT scores, College Board requirements) is mandatory in the allocation of federal college support. By including only the most selective colleges, federal policy reinforces essentially private and expensive institutions. By including all of the approximately 5,400 institutions currently eligible for federal support, federal policy reinforces the least viable educational and social arrangements. The selectivity criterion should be used to include the broadest range of colleges and universities consistent with the perpetuation of meaningful educational standards.

The argument for selectivity rests precisely upon the inability of higher education to carry out the vast, and often contradictory, social, political, and economic promises made in the 1960s. Consequently, it is imperative that we preserve the integrity of higher education by preserving those qualities unique to institutions creating and disseminating knowledge. If we must deny maximum federal support to our better colleges and universities, the cutoff points should at least be generous enough to include a broad array of institutions. A recommended policy rule of thumb is that all universities, comprehensive colleges and universities, and highly selective liberal arts colleges should be eligible for federal support based on the selectivity criterion. As of 1973, these institutions included about 30 percent of all American colleges and universities. However, they enrolled about 70 percent of all college students. By contrast, unselective liberal arts colleges, public community colleges, and private two-year colleges have academic standards inferior to what is reasonably expected in college work.

This proposal is designed to differentiate quality higher education from other types of open-access, vocational, and proprietary arrangements. Against charges of elitism, it must be said that this proposition is designed to restore the integrity of higher education. The economic benefits that students seek through various postsecondary enterprises are beyond the purview of what traditional colleges and universities can reasonably be expected to deliver. In fact, experience with open-access formulas demonstrates the perpetuation of pseudo-equality. Falsely raising the expectations of students from the bottom half of their high school class leads to either dashed hopes or a token degree that conveys the appearance, but not the substance, of genuine college instruction.

Moreover, the postsecondary expansion can no longer pretend that it has the capacity to assure social and economic mobility. This fact was the subject of controversy among a critical minority during the overdevelopment of the 1960s. In light of current economic contraction, it is patently clear that better jobs and social advancement cannot be delivered by postsecondary arrangements.

The inclusion of college selectivity in national higher education policy fulfills the public interest only if it is tied to the spiraling cost of college attendance. That is why federal support should be tied to a second criterion of aid, namely, instructional charges to entering students. This second policy element would maximize federal aid to colleges and universities with the lowest fees and tuitions. The public interest is best served by making a college education available to all meritorious students, regardless of economic class. Federal aid could be an effective incentive to colleges and universities attempting to hold the line on student fees and tuitions. Moreover, there is wide agreement that national policy is responsible for ensuring broad educational opportunity.

The details of this cost provision could be negotiated with the American Council on Education and other higher education interest groups. One procedure is a matching formula in which restraint exercised by institutions concerning student fees is rewarded by additional federal dollars. Another version would have federal support inversely related to the level of college fees. Whatever the specifics, it is imperative that national higher education policy ensure that qualified students are not denied opportunity because the colleges are caught in a spiral of accelerating inflation and fees.

By combining the selectivity and cost planks into a coherent aid program, the national government could maximize opportunity for the best available college education at the lowest price. In general, the most selective colleges and universities tend to be the most expensive. Conversely, the least selective, public, postsecondary institutions tend to be the least expensive. The merit-cost policy for distributing federal institutional aid would have the greatest impact in the broad middle range of colleges and universities. These institutions tend to provide a good education, and their costs are within the capacity of large numbers of students. On the other hand, colleges that are either unselective or expensive would not benefit from this reform in the distribution of federal institutional support.

All Students Are Not Equal

The federal policy for institutional aid must be directly linked to a congruent student aid policy. At present, federal student aid policy is meshed with issues of loans versus scholarships, the criteria and level of requisite need, and the merits of particular programs, such as Basic Educational Opportunity Grants and state supplemental stipends. The clear mandate in existing federal policy is to treat all students as equal with regard to their postsecondary aspirations. Between 1963 and 1972, the number of institutions for which federal student aid was available doubled—from about 2,600 to about 5,200. Most of the bulge consisted of nontraditional postsecondary additions to the collegiate structure. Community colleges, vocational schools, and proprietary institutions were in the vanguard after the 1965 Higher Education Act. Consequently, the new wave of students demanded and received federal support for their education.

A student's financial need ought to be a criterion of federal support. This position is consistent with the enhancement of educational opportunity as a core element in national policy. Indeed, current practices are too restrictive in determining student support and eligibility. For example, certain family assets, such as the value of a residence and the income of a working mother, ought to be excluded in computing the parental contribution to college attendance.

There is also wide agreement that support levels are too low in some cases. For example, Basic Educational Opportunity Grants have never amounted to more than $1,400—individual grants have often been less than that amount because of insufficient funding. Of course, more substantial student aid packages are available by combining several types of support for which students are eligible. Nevertheless, the thrust of federal student aid policy has been in the direction of the open-access system. The cost limitation of the Basic Educational Opportunity Grants discriminates against students from low-income families who attend relatively low-cost public institutions, and against students from lower-middle-income families who attend public community colleges, in the sense that their grants are either very sharply or appreciably reduced below the amounts to which the students would be entitled without the cost limitation. On the other hand, students who are at the upper end of the income range eligible for grants are not affected at all by the cost limitation.

Consequently, the prevailing student aid policy is unintentionally discriminating in two respects. First, it provides less to students at public community colleges than to recipients at more costly universities and four-year colleges. Second, and of greater consequence, the federal student aid policy maldistributes resources to students with lower academic aptitudes, many of whom are concentrated in the open-access system. The logic of suggested national policy reforms is that primary emphasis should be placed on the more academically inclined students and institutions.

However, federal student aid policy should not be limited merely to fiscal need. That policy would merely perpetuate the practice of matching unselective students with unselective institutions. Consequently, the second criterion of federal student aid should be the selectivity of the college or university an individual is attending. Clearly, this is a more controversial proposition than the accepted idea of awarding student aid according to fiscal need. However, it would match the proposed college aid criteria in making academic quality and opportunity, regardless of fiscal status, the paramount considerations.

Institutional and student grants are commonly linked in Britain and Western Europe, where national control of higher education is more pervasive than in the United States. For example, Britain's University Grants Committee—a conduit for national policy—calculates university allotments in terms of student numbers and student grants. The prevailing continental practice is to tie student and institutional grants together in terms of national policy. For example, when the British Labour government decided to bolster the public higher education sector (polytechnics, colleges of education, colleges of further education), both institutional funds and the size of individual student grants were increased.

The idea of differentiating the size of individual student grants in terms of national higher education policy makes good sense. Of course, there will never be political or educational consensus about national priorities within the heterogeneous and decentralized American system. Nevertheless, granting larger awards to needy students attending relatively selective colleges is justified for at least two reasons.

First, academic excellence is one constant and positive goal of American higher education. Specific governmental projects and social missions come and go. The idea of a university as a center of creative and continued learning endures beyond transient political, social, and economic issues. Second, the allocation of student aid tied to college selectivity reinforces the idea of merit and achievement in higher education. It also shifts federal policy from an unworkable welfare concept to essentially collegiate standards of aid distribution. The evidence of the last decade supports the notion that governmental education policy is ineffective as applied social welfare. Therefore, it is necessary to restore the autonomy and viability of American colleges and universities. Qualitative judgments about higher education are made by those within the academic community and its supportive environment. Restructuring the criteria of federal student aid helps to restore the independent processes of American universities, after years of direct positive and negative involvement with governmental policies.

Nontraditional Postsecondary Education Is Different

The policy proposals for reforming national institutional and student support clearly differentiate between traditional higher education and nontraditional postsecondary education. The inclusion of a college's selectivity in awarding direct student support appears to run against the grain of equalitarian strides in providing continued education for all who desire it. In fact, the proposals taking college tuition and student finances into account do fulfill the mandate to provide educational opportunity regardless of economic circumstances.

It is also the case that the Hobbesian necessities facing colleges and universities hard pressed for resources dictate some sensible way of allocating national higher education support. Certainly, the proposals advocated are soundly reasoned, although no one would claim that they are the only way to deal with the situation at hand.

Nevertheless, there is a more fundamental issue at hand, since the proposed reforms do discriminate against community colleges and other open-access or unselective institutions. On this ground, it is certainly the case that the contemplated reform of national policy does move in inequalitarian directions. The fundamental issue is the extent to which many postsecondary institutions provide qualitatively distinct advanced education. And if they do not provide advanced education, are there compensating social, economic, or political factors that dictate continuation of scarce federal higher education support? As David Brenneman and Chester Finn have pointed out:

> It should go without saying that the more heavily the man-
> agers of governmental research and other categorical pro-
> grams rely on academic excellence and scholarly merit in
> their funding decisions, the better they will serve the long-
> term interests of the nation's leading universities, public
> as well as private. That axiom smacks of elitism, but it
> bears repeating because the academic community is not
> always as forthright as it might be in favoring excellence
> over democracy in funding decisions, and government agen-
> cies are under heavy pressure to distribute their funds
> more evenly. [28]

The root of the difficulty about postsecondary expansion is that it sought to solve socioeconomic problems by educational means. It is now clear that no amount of open-access, community college, or proprietary schooling touches the structural problems of unemployment and the barriers to mobility within American society. The decline in economic differentiation between postsecondary and high school graduates, especially among skilled workers, is likely to continue for some time. Moreover, there are fewer professional or managerial positions available for the majority of postsecondary graduates. Future government policy regarding postsecondary schooling can no longer rely upon an expanding pool of high-status and well-paying jobs in the labor market.

The disutility of postsecondary education among marginal groups is reinforced by the positive relationship between college selectivity and the probabilities of social and economic advancement. Perhaps prestige is a more comprehensive term to describe the selective colleges than is high academic admissions and graduation standards.

There is a hierarchy of American colleges and universities, ranging from membership in the national university guild and the highly prestigious liberal arts confederation to the community colleges and other open-access institutions at the bottom of the pyramid. Opportunities for social and economic advancement are positively related to the collegiate ranking system. The relative advantages of the best and the brightest students from the most prestigious institutions are muted in times of economic growth because there are enough surplus jobs and social benefits to satisfy the rising expectations of postsecondary graduates. However, in times of economic and social distress, the relative advantages of membership in the national university guild assume more significant proportions. The graduates of the newer postsecondary institutions become the last ones hired, and first fired, insofar as long-term, good job prospects are concerned. This must result in an intense frustration of recently heightened expectations, and in the possibility of new social and economic distress.

There is an important lesson to be learned from this development. Contrary to some views about the economic and social advantages of postsecondary education, a strong case can be made that higher education is primarily dependent upon political and economic patronage in the broad sense of the term. The higher education expansion during the 1960s was strongly influenced by the needs of government and private enterprise for the contributions supplied by university economy, and government policies, such as Lyndon Johnson's Great Society, generated both the desire and the surplus resources with which to expand and utilize the educational sector.

Indeed, there was a clear progression in the distribution of governmental and corporate support on both the national and state levels. Major research-oriented universities tended to benefit first in support distribution; typically, the expansion then moved to the state college level, and then to the two-year institutions. Moreover, the flow of resources followed a comparable trickle-down pattern with respect to broad fields of academic study. The initial strong commitment was made to science, technology, and medicine as early as 1958, with the passage of the National Defense Education Act. Social science support and prestige rose sharply during the 1960s in response to acute racial and urban stress, and to the new claims of scientific knowledge, made by social scientists, that purported to solve these problems. The fusion of knowledge and money was finally completed among the arts and humanities—for example, the establishment of national endowments for the arts and the humanities.

The idea that higher education depends upon the support of a patron also suggests that, unlike the business corporation, colleges and universities produce mostly indeterminate products. All our experience with government-contract research and job prospects for college graduates should not obscure the fact that the ultimate value of knowledge is an intangible social benefit. Whatever the overstated claims of the past, the foundation of higher education support rests on the value the community places on an intangible social asset. Consequently, the present claim of higher education for public support is ultimately based upon the value public patrons (state governments, the Department of Health, Education and Welfare, and so on) place on tangible returns.

In essence, colleges and universities cannot now satisfy past claims about solving the problems of social mobility, employment, and equality. The wise course of action is to retain the intellectual mission that colleges and universities are capable of fulfilling. The response to the government patron then becomes an acknowledgment of human and institutional limitations, coupled with reliance upon the historical function of higher education as a creator and disseminator of knowledge.

This is not to suggest that the national government should ignore the claims and aspirations of the new postsecondary population. Indeed, it is imperative to recognize that their problems cannot be dealt with effectively within the traditional structure of American higher education. Rather than destroying our hard-pressed viable colleges and universities, we need to devise ways of treating the roots of economic and social distress.

This requires that we understand and act upon the difference between a social policy and a social program. A social policy is designed to alleviate the root causes of a problem. By contrast, a social program merely deals with symptoms of a problem. A social policy is comprehensive; a social program is narrow and one-dimensional.

From a broad policy perspective, the national government must ensure that higher education opportunities are available to all who desire them. It is the availability of educational opportunities per se that differentiates support to colleges and students from other types of federal welfare policies. By contrast, expanding a narrow program, such as community colleges and Basic Educational Opportunity Grants, undermines policy by confusing educational and socioeconomic goals and means.

The postsecondary educational structure is presently inappropriate to the employment, opportunity, and welfare needs of many of our citizens. Consequently, it is of utmost importance that other federal social and economic agencies undertake the responsibilities currently misappropriated to the postsecondary educational sector. While the specific suggestions offered in Chapter 5 may be useful here, the ultimate solution of socioeconomic problems is best dealt with by policy experts in those fields, not by educators. The policy agenda of higher education is difficult enough without clouding the issue. Therefore, the most educationally effective means is a program of continuing education that enables everyone to pursue all the learning he can profitably absorb.

How is this concept consistent with the repeated claim that national higher education policy ought not invest in the academically unselective postsecondary system? One essential element is the difference between the credentialing and the avocational uses of higher education. The postsecondary expansion resulted in the creation of separate institutional structures (state college systems, community colleges, open-access schools) within the pyramid of American colleges and universities. The subsequent mass awarding of cheap degrees—credentialing without substantive advanced learning or improved socioeconomic status—contributed to the contemporary crisis in national policy.

Consequently, it is imperative that continuing education, distinct from degrees and unrealistic economic expectations, be supported by public and private agencies. A variety of arrangements are possible—for example, the bolstering of adult-oriented, continuing education centers on major college campuses. The national government could help by devoting some funds to the continuing education programs. This effort, and the viability of Washington's contribution to a reformed higher education policy, would be augmented if a separate National Foundation for Higher Education were established and funded. Whatever the specific arrangements, the main task is to concentrate on the delivery of intrinsic educational services.

To summarize, an integrated national policy would take the following steps:

1. delegate vocational, proprietary, and nontraditional secondary education functions to other agencies, such as the Departments of Labor and Commerce, more capable of dealing with the basic socioeconomic issues;
2. continue a policy that makes higher education possible regardless of economic class—students with fiscal needs, and colleges and universities with low fees and tuitions, deserve maximum support;
3. preserve the unique qualities of genuinely advanced learning by maximizing federal support of academically selective students and colleges;
4. integrate programs of student and institutional support into a coherent, broad-gauged national higher education policy;
5. support nondegree continuing education programs in colleges and universities capable of providing adult-oriented instruction; the desire to learn would replace an essentially dead-end, postsecondary sector currently stalled at the bottom of the university pyramid.

NOTES

1. Daniel P. Moynihan, Coping: On the Practice of Government (New York: Random House, 1973), p. 308.

2. Arnold J. Heidenheimer and Michael Parkinson, "Equalizing Educational Opportunity in Britain and the United States," Tulane Studies in Political Science 15 (1972).

3. Stephen K. Bailey, "Education and the State," mimeographed (Washington, D. C.: The American Council on Education, 1973), p. 7.

4. Joel Spring, The Sorting Machine: National Educational Policy Since 1954 (New York: David McKay, 1976), pp. 261-62.

5. Earl Cheit, The New Depression in Higher Education (Berkeley: Carnegie Commission on Higher Education, 1971), p. 5.

6. Carnegie Foundation for the Advancement of Teaching, More Than Survival (San Francisco: Jossey-Bass, 1975), p. 2.

7. Martin Trow, "The Public and Private Lives of Higher Education," Daedalus 104, no. 2 (1975): 113-27.

8. Martin Trow, "Notes on American Higher Education," Higher Education 4 (1975): 10.

9. Ibid.

10. Earl Cheit, The New Depression in Higher Education—Two Years Later (Berkeley: Carnegie Commission on Higher Education, 1973), p. 64.

11. Ibid., p. 67.

12. Ibid., p. 69.

13. Carnegie Foundation for the Advancement of Teaching, op. cit.

14. Nathan Glazer, Affirmative Discrimination: Ethnic Inequality and Public Policy (New York: Basic Books, 1975), pp. 196-97.

15. This section draws on material in Edgar Litt, "Successes and Failures of Equal Educational Opportunity Programs in the United States," Proceedings, British Society for Research into Higher Education (London), 1974, pp. 69-74.

16. U. S. Department of Labor, Order No. 4, 1965. The Department of Health, Education, and Welfare's affirmative action enforcement program is derived from authority delegated to it by the Labor Department.

17. White House Office, Executive Order No. 11375, 1967.

18. U. S. Department of Labor, Order No. 11375, 1967.

19. Glazer, op. cit., pp. 58-59.

20. George La Noue, "Status of Women in the Profession: Grievances" (Paper read at the annual meetings of the American Political Science Association, New Orleans, September, 1973), pp. 10-11.

21. Carnegie Council on Policy Studies in Higher Education, Making Affirmative Action Work in Higher Education (San Francisco: Jossey-Bass, 1975), p. 14.

22. Carnegie Council on Policy Studies in Higher Education, op. cit.

23. Glazer, op. cit. , pp. 205.

24. Thomas Sewell, "Affirmative Action Reconsidered," The Public Interest, no. 42, Winter 1976, pp. 47-65.

25. Ibid. , p. 61.

26. Ibid. , p. 63.

27. Quoted in The Chronicle of Higher Education, October 9, 1976, p. 9. In 1977, President Carter recommended $2. 3 billion for BEOG—about half the supplementary education funding that was allocated in the budget of the outgoing Ford administration. The fundable maximum individual grant increased from $1,400 to $1,600 per student. An additional half-million students from families with incomes in the $13-$17,000 range became eligible for basic opportunity grants.

28. David Brenneman and Chester Finn, eds. , Public Policy and Private Higher Education (Washington, D. C. : Brookings Institution, 1978), p. 458.

PART II

HIGHER EDUCATION: POLICY LEVELING

INTRODUCTION

The expansion of higher education in the 1960s, on both sides of the Atlantic, soon gave way to the need for efficiency combined with equality. Consequently, the growth rate of universities and other post-secondary institutions was slowed down significantly after 1970. This underscores the conflict between the classic liberal view of educational opportunity, which requires that additional resources be pumped into the system in order to eradicate discrimination and inequality, and the managerial viewpoint, which demands the most rational and efficient use of existing resources as the sine qua non of university governance. The irony is that the differences between equalitarian and economizing tendencies were in fact harmonized in the new policy.

For example, in the United States, the shift of federal resources from direct college aid to student aid was supported by a curious alliance of equalitarians in Congress, who were demanding more minority-group opportunity, and the conservative Nixon-Ford administrations, who were primarily concerned with aid to the poor, but also with maintaining a market level of college tuition and fees for the rest of society. The result was the expansive Basic Educational Opportunity Grant program of 1972, which provides sufficient aid only for relatively unselective, and low-cost, institutions. In Britain, the shift of resources from the universities to the polytechnics was also justified on the grounds of economy and equality. But the results were quite different from either of these expectations. For example, as polytechnics increased in status and size, their unit student costs approached those of the more expensive, and traditionally better-endowed, universities.

Moreover, British working-class participation, which traditionally had been greatest in institutions offering part-time and joint work-college programs, declined as these institutions became more like universities, in their existing form and their aspirations, and became more interested in research than in teaching, and more concerned about full-time students than about part-time students. In fact, the binary policy, designed to aid the working-class students by elevating the polytechnics, has not expanded the opportunities of this largest social stratum for participating in British higher education.

The quest for equality on economic grounds has presented other policy difficulties. For example, the widespread use of relatively cheaper community colleges obviously provided more opportunity in many American state systems. However, the dropout rate was so enormous that the fruits of open-access education were severely damaged. Obviously policy makers can become victims of social illusions as readily as anyone else. The belief that cheaper education represents equality has been especially strong in the retrenchment years of the 1970s. There is also a strong relationship between this kind of policy leveling and the centralization of government power over higher education. It is no accident that universities were the retrenched establishments in the eyes of both the British Department of Education and Science, and the assorted federal and state higher education agencies in the United States.

The fusion between efficiency and equality, which stimulated recent policy shifts, is deeply rooted in both cultures. The Fabian belief that social justice and sound management can be wedded infuses the intellectual history of the British Labour Party. In America, management efficiency is strongly emphasized in industrial-relations, business-school, and public administration programs. Moreover, these views are easily adapted to more equalitarian notions of democracy and justice. In the end, professional bureaucrats have become the social group most capable, in their own eyes, of serving as the twin engines of social and administrative change.

4

POLICY LEVELING IN BRITAIN

Prior to 1960, Britain had one of the lowest rates of university attendance in Western Europe. Indeed, compared with the situation in the United States and on the continent, middle-class demand for university education was relatively limited. As Anthony Sampson has observed:

> Going to universities is a much more solid ambition among the sons of the bourgeoisie in France or Germany than in Britain and many of the British middle class have tended to be skeptical, if not actually hostile, to university education for their children. [1]

And no other country's universities had been dominated for six centuries in the way that Oxford and Cambridge had dominated British education and controlled the heights of intellectual life as well as access to the centers of political, cultural, and economic power.

It is true that the Victorian foundation, or redbrick universities, provided quality university education in London, the midlands, and the industrial north. Nevertheless, the premodern notion of liberal arts for the elite dominated British intellectual and scientific life. This meant that a British university—more particularly, an English university—was evaluated in terms of normative criteria quite different from those employed by the continental Europeans or the Americans. The British university ideal, Halsey suggests, should have these characteristics:

> First, it should be ancient; second, it should draw its students, not from a restricted regional locality, but from the nation and internationally; third, its students, whatever their origins, should be carefully selected as likely to fit into and maintain the established life and character of the

university; fourth, those who enter should be offered (to
use a Victorian distinction) "education" and not merely
"training." This end necessitates, fifth, a small-scale
residential community affording close contact of teachers
and students in a shared domestic life and, sixth, a high
staff-student ratio for individualized teaching. [2]

When universities expanded in the 1960s, many of the new institutions were located in cathedral towns. While university expansion
could have been directed to supplement the urban redbrick workhorses
of the system in Leeds and Manchester, London and Birmingham, this
proved unlikely. And the accidents of history prevented the new additions to British university life from being located at Oxford and Cambridge. Consequently, with the new institutions located in cathedral
towns, the style of British university life continued to reflect the historic norms, and their cultivation at Oxford and Cambridge. British
universities have been predominantly undergraduate institutions, as
contrasted with the German and American models. The tutorial,
whether at Oxford or Sheffield, is to British university life what the
seminar is to the American graduate school, and what the lecture is
to the Free University of Berlin.

The strength of these characteristics is formidable. And when
in the mid-1960s, the Labour government unveiled its binary policy
of raising technical institutions and education to equal status with the
universities, it represented a quite un-British effort to accommodate
vocational training and involve the business community in higher education:

It was only after France and Germany had founded their
polytechniques and hochschulen for technomanagers that
Britain gradually felt the need to adapt their universities
to technical education. . . . They were designed, not like
the Continental schools to produce a separate scientific
culture, but to bring the new world of technology closer to
the old world of liberal education. [3]

The governance of British universities reinforced their basic
values. Unlike the case of the newer polytechnics or the colleges of
education, local government exercises no financial controls or regulations over the universities. Rather, support from the national
government accounted for up to 85 percent of university funding, free-
ing higher learning from both local and external influences, such as
the power of big business that has influenced, for example, the history
of the University of Chicago or of Columbia University. Moreover,
the unique University Grants Committee prevented the piper from

calling the academic tune. Funds from the Treasury went to the UGC, and this governmental body, largely composed of university men, allocated funds on the basis of preestablished criteria. Consequently, there was a fair standard for allocating both university and student grants on the basis of accepted educational criteria. It was this rule "of the dons, by the dons, and for the dons" that helped perpetuate a national system with shared academic values and practices.

But the Robbins report of 1963, with its call for the expansion of British universities, may be read as the last advocacy of these ancient liberal values regarding university education. Thereafter, the language of bureaucratic efficiency, the call for more resources devoted to technical studies, and plans to expand central control over funding and programs became the order of the day. Since as late as 1965, only 12 percent of the relevant British age cohort attended universities, compared with 40 percent in the United States; the demands of a modern labor market and political economy left little time for the sentiments of the Oxford college arrangement. Indeed, since the 1960s, events have unfolded rapidly, and the world of higher education has experienced a sea change.

THE GOLDEN AGE, 1963-72

Government policy for higher education in Britain since the 1960s falls into two distinct periods. The first was a period of rapid expansion of institutions and opportunities, which lasted from the early 1960s until the issuing of the Conservative government's white paper on education in 1972. In the five years between 1962 and 1967, for example, the number of students in full-time higher education increased by 75 percent, from 193,000 to 339,000. The increase in the absolute number of undergraduates was greater than the increase over the previous 50 years, and almost twice as great as that in the immediately preceding five years. The percentage of the age groups in higher education rose from 8 percent to 14 percent between 1960 and 1967.[4] The second policy phase, engineered since 1972 by both Conservative and Labour governments, demonstrates the impact of the new centralized decision-making system, as governments have sought to restrain expansion and to combine the goals of social justice and economy. Continued growth is still planned for the higher education sector, but at a significantly lower rate than that intended during the 1960s. The new policy has been developed collectively by both major political parties and the DES, in the face of intense criticism by many groups involved in both the providing and receiving of higher education.

After World War II a variety of social, economic, and political forces had combined to generate increased demand for higher education. In 1963 the Conservative government created the Robbins Committee to inquire into all aspects of higher education in Britain. [5] In keeping with the spirit of the many reformist, expansionist reports of the period, Robbins recommended that individual demand be the primary criterion for the provision of an expanded number of places in higher education. Specifically, it set a target of 510,000 places in higher education for the year 1981-82. The committee's report and targets were accepted within a day by the government. In fact, as many observers at the time recognized, Robbins's estimates proved to be too conservative, primarily because of their failure to anticipate the growth, throughout the 1960s, of the percentage of the age group qualified to enter higher education. As a result, successive governments had to revise upward the Robbins estimates until 1972, as Table 4.1 shows. The 1970 figure of 835,000 places required for 1981, represents the highest projection ever made by the DES. But since then, governments have steadily retreated from that figure. In 1972 the figure of 750,000 was substituted by the Conservative government. By 1976 the Labour government had reduced its target for places in higher education to 600,000. Changes in policies then flowed from these changing projections.

British higher education evolved from an elitist, class-based orientation, typified by Oxbridge, with its strong reliance on perpetuating the dominant ruling class. The thrust of American higher education points in the opposite direction, namely, mass expansion of educational opportunity, dating back to the creation of land-grant colleges in the nineteenth century. At present, only about 15 percent of British youth attend some postsecondary institutions, compared to about four times that percentage among the comparable American population.

The implementation of the Robbins report was very much in the British educational tradition of meritocratic adjustment. The number of secondary school graduates qualified for university places had risen sharply, when measured by performance in public examinations. Clearly, many more students could perform in British universities than actually entered. There was also a social demand, led by the expanding British middle class. In fact, cynics point out that the Robbins report was acted on to satisfy the growing professional class, whose sons and daughters could not study at Oxford or Cambridge, and who sought an updated education at similarly prestigious schools. The cynics overstate the case, although the children of senior civil servants and university professors did attend the new universities in considerable numbers. And it was not the first time that social reform had benefited the professional class—in this case, the sons and daughters of the reformers.

But the most important point regarding the expansion is the continuity of higher education policy within the British context. The stu-

TABLE 4.1

Total Places in Full-Time Higher Education in England and Wales
(000s)

Year	Universities	Colleges of Education	Institutions of Advanced Education	Total	Average Annual Percentage Increase over Preceding Period	Robbins Projection
1961 (actual number)	102.5	36.6	23.8	162.9	—	162.9
1967 (actual number)	167.6	97.1	66.0	330.7	12.5	280.8
1971 (projected number)	215.6	118.0	103.2	436.8	7.2	304.9
1976 (projected number)	286.9	124.2	146.3	557.4	5.0	387.5
1981 (projected number)	394.4	129.6	203.1	727.1	5.5	510.0

Note: In 1970, the DES was not responsible for Scottish universities or higher education. It estimated the following, however, for Britain: 1981 (projected number) 460,000 375,000 835,000 54.1 44.5 100

Source: Department of Education and Science, Student Numbers in Higher Education, Planning Paper, no. 2, (London: Her Majesty's Stationery Office, 1970).

dents of the 1960s were located in the cathedral towns of York and
Canterbury, rather than in the urban sprawl of greater London and the
west midlands, because of the association of university life with clas-
sical, preindustrial values. Despite the considerable influx of bright
working-class youngsters into the plate-glass universities, as the new
institutions were called, these became neither working-class nor vocational institutions. Indeed, British universities have never been
working-class institutions; they are highly selective, shaped by a history of academic tradition and social realities in a society where 65
percent of the labor force are skilled, semiskilled, and unskilled
workers.

Although the recommended rapid rate of expansion was the primary theme of the Robbins report's many proposals, its recommendation that higher education should be contained within a single administrative framework was dominated by the ideal of the liberal university.
The expansion was to take place within the existing institutional pattern. There was felt to be no need for new kinds of institutions to cater
to more vocational kinds of education, or to the relatively under-priv-
ileged fields of applied technology, or indeed to the different kind of
student that might, in the future, be expected to enter higher education for the first time.

In essence, the Robbins report fostered liberal education and
the idea of a university as responses to problems of a technocratic
era:

> Insofar as it based its case on the inherent value of ex-
> pansion rather than upon economic demands, the Robbins
> report represents possibly the last "liberal" document
> that a government will produce for some time. Robbins
> says that universities must emphasize the common ele-
> ments in civilizations rather than the minor variations.
> . . . Despite his modernity, the essence of Robbins' con-
> cept of a university community is very similar to the aris-
> tocratic tradition which Cardinal Newman extolled: it is
> the fostering of a common identity that is all important in
> higher education. [6]

THE BINARY SYSTEM, 1965-72

After 1965 the Labour government departed from the Robbins
philosophy and instituted the so-called binary system, which rests
on a distinction between the autonomous university sector, financed
but only loosely controlled by the central government through the University Grants Committee, and the public sector, consisting of poly-

technics and colleges, financed and controlled directly by the DES and
the local education authorities. In the view of the Labour government,
the public sector—primarily the 30 polytechnics created after 1965—
was to offer university-level education in socially relevant disciplines,
especially the applied technologies, to students conventionally excluded
from the socially and academically exclusive universities, essentially
the working classes. British universities have never reflected the so-
cial-class composition of the country as a whole, as the Robbins research showed clearly. Since the 1920s, for example, the proportion
of university students with working-class parents had remained constant at 25 percent. There is little evidence to suggest any significant
changes have occurred in the decade following the Robbins research.
By contrast, the institutions that were merged into the polytechnics
had catered more overtly to working-class students—34 percent of
students enrolled in full-time advanced courses had working-class
parents, and the proportion in courses combining work and education
was 44 percent. Part-time students in these colleges consisted of about
60 percent working-class students. [7]

The binary policy was designed to upgrade the status of the underprivileged technological programs, and their students, to that of the
universities. Direct public control was thought to be necessary in order
that the polytechnics, unlike the universities, would become socially
responsive both in the range of studies they offered and the students
they would recruit. Also unlike the universities, the polytechnics were
not permitted to award their own degree. A new institution, the Council for National Academic Awards, was created to validate externally
the courses and qualifications offered in the polytechnics, stressing,
once again, their public accountability.

The binary policy marked a sharp departure from the Robbins
philosophy. As we have seen, the Robbins report attempted to direct
old liberal notions to a new technocratic and remedial program. One
of the deliberate intentions of the Robbins Committee was to foster
university orientations and to abolish rigid structural differences. The
university sector was to expand most, but other institutions were capable of either university status—as indeed was the case with colleges
of advanced technology—or making links with existing universities.

These propositions overlooked the fact that further education is
inextricably tied to large numbers of part-time courses, so unless
part-timers are to be included within the university orbit, they would
be relegated to second-class status. Moreover, in putting forth an expansive, university-oriented system, the Robbins Committee assumed
that the government was willing and able to pay for its proposals,
which would have raised higher education expenditures threefold between 1962 and 1981.

Whereas the supreme principle of the Robbins report was that there should be no rigid distinction between types of institutions in higher education, the binary system involved the segregation of institutions into two completely discrete compartments. While Robbins encouraged a unitary culture, the binary system is based on the fundamental gulf between theoretical and applied knowledge, and between the abstract and the practical. While Robbins sought to meet technocratic problems by broadening the university tradition, the binary system reflected the problem of encouraging a technocratic ethos against the old liberal monopoly of the universities. While the Robbins proposals meant expansion and significant new costs, the binary system can be rationalized to provide, as cheaply as possible, middle- and lower-grade technicians for the economy and teachers for the schools.

Anthony Crosland's articulation of the original binary scheme accentuates the fundamental policy change:

> On the one hand we have what has come to be called the autonomous sector, represented by the universities, in whose hands, of course, I now include the Colleges of Advanced Technology. On the other hand, we have the public sector, represented by the leading technical colleges and Colleges of Education. The government accepts this dual system as being fundamentally the right one, with each sector making its own distinctive contribution to the whole.

> We prefer the dual system for four basic reasons. First, there is an ever increasing need and demand for vocational, professional and industrially-based courses in higher education. This demand cannot be fully met by the universities. It therefore requires a separate sector with a separate tradition and outlook. Secondly, if the universities have a "class" monopoly as degree giving bodies and if every college which achieves high standards moves automatically into the university club, then the residual public sector becomes a permanent poor relation. This must be bad for morale, bad for standards, and productive only of an unhealthy rat-race mentality.

> Thirdly, it is desirable in itself that a substantial part of the higher education system should be under social control, directly responsible to social needs. Fourthly, why should we not aim at a vocationally-oriented non-university sector which is degree giving and with an appropriate amount of post-graduate work and opportunities for learning

comparable with those of the universities, and giving a
first-class professional training? Between these sectors
we want mutual understanding and healthy rivalry where
their work overlaps.

The polytechnics will provide full-time and part-time
courses for students of university quality who are attracted by the more vocational tradition of the colleges,
and who are more interested in applying knowledge to the
solution of problems than in pursuing learning for its own
sake. [8]

The binary system was dogged by criticism and confusion from the
start. Critics accused it, alternatively, of devaluing the universities,
sustaining a cheap, inferior education for the working classes, or,
more neutrally, of being administratively irrational.

Original criticism of the binary system dwelt upon the likely
second-class status of the public sector. Lord Robbins, himself, made
this critique of the Labour Party's scheme: "I can sincerely say that
nothing has astonished me more than that a government with an equalitarian background and actively engaged at the school level in an attempt to reduce unnecessary and invidious distinctions, should be en-
ergetically supporting, in the field of higher education, a separation
which must have exactly the opposite effect. "[9]

Of late, the line of attack against the public sector has shifted.
Recent criticism concentrates on the fact that the polytechnics, in a
search for university status, have not carried out their original intended function, by neglecting important subdegree work, shedding
part-time courses and students, and by seeking to become more research oriented rather than purely teaching institutions.

THE CONSERVATIVES AND RETRENCHMENT—THE 1972
WHITE PAPER

It should be observed that in the period from the inception of the
binary system in 1965 until 1972, although policy makers stressed the
contributions of polytechnics to both higher education and the national
economy, relatively few funds were made available to them. As a result, they remained underprivileged institutions, especially in relation to the universities. Since then, both political parties, when in
power, have begun to allocate added resources to the public sector.
In its concern to cut higher education costs by expanding the allegedly
cheaper polytechnics, the Conservative government legitimized and
transformed the binary system. The change from the expansionist

policies of the 1960s was signaled by the publication in 1972 of the
Conservative government's white paper on education, the first product
of the new decision-making system. It introduced a new style in both
policies and policy making, in a new era of austerity and rationalization. Essentially, the new policy abandoned the ideological optimism
of the Robbins report. In specific terms, it marked a retreat from
the peak projections for the 1970s made by the DES in 1970. The new
emphasis was on rationalization of commitments and the diversion of
funds away from the privileged sector of higher education and toward
more socially deserving areas of the education service, like nursery
schools and improved in-service teacher training. Throughout the
1960s, for example, expenditure on higher education had grown annually by 6.5 percent. In the 1970s, this was to be cut back to 5 percent. Expenditure on the schools, which had increased at the rate of
2.5 percent during the 1960s, was, by contrast, to rise at an annual
rate of 3 percent in the 1970s.

But equally significant, within higher education itself, resources
were to be channeled away from the privileged university sector and
into the underprivileged and apparently cheaper public sector, especially the polytechnics. The basis for this decision was the DES's cal-
culation in its 1970 planning paper that the average combined capital
and current cost of educating a university student was £1,625 a year,
as opposed to £1,120 for a student doing comparable full-time, ad-
vanced-level work in the public sector. The total number of projected
places for Britain for 1981 was reduced from the 835,000 calculated
in the 1970 planning paper to 750,000. But all of the shortfall of 85,000
was to be experienced by the universities. The polytechnics were to
continue to expand at the 1970 rate—much more rapidly than any other
part of the sector, as Table 4.2 shows.

The 1972-77 quinquennial settlement revealed that the universities were to suffer in other respects. The number of graduate students requested by the UGC was cut by 7,000. Limits were imposed
on staff expansion. Only 8,270 new teaching posts, instead of the
11,850 the UGC had requested for the 1972-77 quinquennium, were
allocated. Similarly, 1,300 fewer promotions than had been planned
by the UGC were authorized during the period. Given the planned rate
of expansion for the universities, these reductions meant that unit
costs per university student were reduced about 25 percent. And it
has been estimated that in overall terms, the new projections represented a 5 percent cut in opportunities for entry into higher education,
compared with the DES estimates of 1970.[10] Since 1972, estimates
of the need for places in 1981 have been reduced to 600,000, and the
financial pressures on the universities have been maintained.

The white paper contained other suggestions for reducing costs
in higher education that were likely to favor the cheaper polytechnic

TABLE 4. 2

1972 White Paper Projections for Higher Education, 1971-81

Type of Institution	1971	1981	Percent Increase, 1971-81
Universities in Britain	234,000	375,000	60
Polytechnics (England and Wales)	66,000	180,000	190
Colleges of education, and colleges of further education (England and Wales)	138,000	150,000	10
Total	440,000	705,000	

Note: The total of 705,000 used in this table excludes nonuniversity higher education in Scotland, for which the DES is not responsible.
Source: The 1972 white paper.

sector, such as a faster rate of growth in provision for part-time students, and an increase in students based at home rather than in expensive residential accommodations. One of the most significant proposals in the document was the introduction of a new, subdegree level of qualification, the two-year diploma of higher education. Although this diploma was partly designed to accommodate new plans for teacher training, it introduced the idea that in the future, large numbers of students would seek a two-year, rather than a conventional three- or four-year, course of study in higher education. Even though it might be valuable to introduce such a program—which was shorter and cheaper, and more flexible, than the conventional degree program— in a period of expansion, when there was demand from those new students who had not traditionally entered higher education, the DES was planning to use the new qualification to channel existing demand into the cheapest route during a period of financial austerity. [11]
So the outlines of a new policy had been made clear by the Conservative government. A loss of confidence in higher education generally meant there were to be reduced resources available to it in the future. Within higher education, the cheaper, socially responsive public sector was to be favored at the expense of the universities. And within the public sector, polytechnics were favored over colleges of education, and colleges of further education. In general, increasing

stress was laid on the need for economy, contraction, and rationalization.

Increased support for the public sector has taken several forms, partly designed to improve the position of the polytechnics, partly to restrict that of the universities. The government has agreed, for example, that both kinds of institutions should have a common student-staff ratio of ten to one, a marked deterioration for the universities and a corresponding improvement for the polytechnics. In 1975, for the first time, the capital expenditure approved for the polytechnics was larger than that for the universities, as shown in Table 4.3. The upgrading of the polytechnics was continued by the Labour government's manipulation of the separate salary structures in the two sectors in 1975 and 1976, which placed polytechnic staff and administrators, for the first time, financially ahead of their counterparts in the universities.

By contrast, the elitist universities, while still dominating higher education in many respects, have increasingly lost the support of poli-

TABLE 4.3

Capital Expenditures for Polytechnics and Universities (millions of pounds)

Year	Polytechnics	Universities
1967–68	7.6	35
1968–69	4.0	25
1969–70	8.5	29
1970–71	5.2	29
1971–72	4.8	50
1972–73	7.3	
1973–74	19.0	35
1974–75	27.0	29
1975–76	20.0	15
1976–77	48.0	14
1977–78	35.0	7

Source: John Pratt and Tyrell Burgess, The Polytechnics (London: Pitman, 1974), p. 113, and The Chronicle of Higher Education, October 11, 1976, p. 2. Reprinted with permission. Copyright 1976 by Editorial Projects for Education, Inc.

TABLE 4.4

Projected Distribution of Public Expenditure, by Major Programs,
for 1977-78
(percent)

Program	Command 5519[a]	Command 5879[b]	Change in Percentage Share
Housing	6.0	10.0	+4.0
Social security	19.5	21.0	+2.0
Agriculture, fish, and forestry (food subsidies)	1.2	2.2	+1.0
Trade, industry, and employment	3.0	3.7	+0.7
Health and personal social services	12.3	11.5	-0.8
Roads and transport	5.6	5.0	-0.6
Defense	11.7	10.6	-1.1
Education, libraries, science, and arts	15.8	13.4	-2.4

[a]White paper, December 1973; calculated at survey prices.
[b]White paper, January 1975; calculated at survey prices.
Source: Times Higher Educational Supplement, January 24,
1975.

ticians and the civil service in the 1970s. They lost it initially under
the Conservative government, as revealed by the policies in the 1972
white paper and the important 1973 white paper on public expenditure,
which led to large cuts in higher education expenditure. But the pressures on the universities intensified with the return of a Labour government in 1974. Indeed, Labour's return to power clearly confirmed
the emergence of a bipartisan consensus on higher education policy in
Britain. Far from changing the policies of their Conservative prede-
cessors, the Labour government has pursued them with increased
vigor. Their principal strategy has been to reduce expenditure on education in general, in order that resources could be transferred to
other social policy areas. This trend can be seen in Table 4.4, which
shows the differences in projected government expenditure between the

Conservative government's 1973 white paper and the white paper produced by Labour in 1975. Education remained a major consumer of public funds, but Labour planned for increased resources to go to housing and social security, and for education to suffer the largest percentage cut in order to finance this redistribution.

Of equal significance, the transfer of resources from the more privileged sector of the educational service to the underprivileged sector has been continued by Labour. The government has identified three broad groups as being the most important in the competition for limited resources: children of compulsory school age; the 16–19 age group, for whom little aid has been traditionally available; and the illiterate. Small but significant sums of money have been allocated to help these target populations.

By contrast, the universities have continued to suffer. Cuts in both capital and recurrent expenditure through 1974, 1975, and 1976 led to many capital projects being abandoned and many new initiatives lost. One thousand posts have been left unfilled in order to help the economic situation. Staff–student ratios have deteriorated. In 1976 cash limits were imposed upon universities for the first time, eliminating any compensation for inflation or unseen costs they might face, and further tightening government constraints on expenditure. In 1977 the universities received £17 million less in spendable income than they were awarded in 1976. The cuts have been particularly damaging to laboratory and library acquisitions, and to the quality of graduate programs.

Moreover, British universities increasingly turn to the marketplace of student fees, thereby resembling their American counterparts. The initial fee impact is on graduate and overseas students, but continued deterioration of the economy must lead to either the imposition of undergraduate tuitions or the enrollment of less qualified students, to ensure that budget allotments—awarded on the basis of enrollments—are not further reduced. Overseas students have already suffered from retrenchment. In the decade since 1967, the number of foreign students in Britain increased from 31,000 to about 80,000. The current cost to the government to support foreign students is about $125 million. University fees for foreign students—£250 a year in 1966—rose to £650 for undergraduates and £850 for graduate students in 1977. Projected further increases will price out immigrants from former British colonies and elsewhere.

Per-student expenditures for the universities and for the public sector are approaching parity—a far cry from the 1961 situation, in which £581 was spent per university student, compared with £249 per student in the public sector. And the universities are losing the battle for enrollments. They enrolled 51 percent of all postsecondary students in 1961, compared with only 42 percent of the total in 1977. Consequently, student fees account for larger shares of university costs. For example, Essex University increased its percentage of operating costs coming directly from students from 9 percent in 1975 to 27 percent in 1977.

Perhaps most serious, quinquennial planning, the very basis of university planning, which has been so attractive to universities, has been eliminated. Universities are now funded on an annual basis, without the certainty they once enjoyed with five years of planning; indeed, they are kept waiting from year to year for government indications of future levels of financial support. Moreover, central control by the minister of state for higher education has also increased in the determination of the spread of disciplines within the universities. Manpower considerations will form a more fundamental aspect of future British policy in higher education.

Indeed, ministers have constantly stressed the elements of university efficiency and economy, combined with the binary policy:

> In essence part of what I have been saying about priorities
> in further and higher education is that in achieving our tar-
> gets higher and further education has got to consider its
> unit cost problems, just as we have in other areas of our
> national life. Just as we have got to become more efficient
> in industry, so we have to improve in education. [12]

Or, as noted in another report:

> It simply will not do to allow universities and polytech-
> nics to produce whatever people they fancy or to relate
> the number and kind of places they provide to the applica-
> tions that come forward. . . . We need to estimate our
> likely future needs for different broad categories of trained
> manpower deriving from the experiences of some of
> our industrial competitors and from their views on differ-
> ent propositions and types of trained manpower they now
> have and are planning for. [13]

The DES has always regarded the integration of higher education as fruitful. During the 1970s it consistently advanced the notion that there should be regional integration of all institutions, with particular emphasis placed upon the need for closer contacts between the universities and the polytechnics. The universities have already rejected such plans for regional integration. But in this sense, the future status of the universities has become increasingly problematic.

In recent years, university salaries have declined more sharply than wages in the public sector, as Table 4.5 demonstrates. Comment-

TABLE 4.5

University/Public Sector Salaries in Relation to Indexes of Weekly Wage Rates and Retail Prices, 1965–75

Year	Weekly Wage Rate Index	Retail Price Index	Public Sector Salaries[c]	University Salaries
1965	100	100[a]	100	100
1966		104.4[a]	113	105
1967		108.1[a]	121.2	105[b]
1968		110.8[a]	121.2	114.5[b]
1969		117.9[a]	128.8	124.8[b]
1970		123.4[a]	136.5	137.2[b]
1971		133.2[a]	150.8	147.5[b]
1972	185[b]	143.4[a]	162.5	158.6[b]
1973	206[b]	153.7[a]	172.3	167.2[b]
1974	254[b]	170.2[a]	234.1 (186.1)	186.0[b]
1975	288	220.2	276.2	236.8[b, d]

[a]January.
[b]October.
[c]Public sector includes polytechnics but not colleges of education.
[d]Minimum, based on a DES offer, July 1975.

Note: All figures are for April except where otherwise noted. The relative percent decline in relation to weekly wage rates, for 1965–75, was 4.1 percent in public sector salaries and 17.8 percent in university salaries. In 1972, average public sector salary was approximately £2,800, and average university salary about £3,700.

Source: David H. McKay, "The Political Response to Fiscal Crisis: The Case of Higher Education in Britain and the U.S." (Paper read at 1975 annual meetings of the American Political Science Association, San Francisco, September 2–5, 1975).

74

ing on this and related developments, David McKay observes: "Government statements urging greater efficiency, economy, and a shift to cheaper, more vocational institutions appear to be evidence of the state not only hoping to pare the costs of higher education, but also trying to make higher education better serve the needs of the productive manufacturing and commercial sectors of the economy."[14]

Moreover, the declining purchasing power of the British student grant most adversely affects the opportunities of poor students for attending the more expensive universities (see Table 4.6). In Britain, every matriculating student is entitled to a grant financed by the central government. The grant is designed to cover fees, travel, book purchases, and living and incidental expenses. There is also a parental contribution, which is means tested and progressive. Lower-income parents pay nothing while higher-income parents are required to pay a substantial part of the grant. The diminished purchasing value

TABLE 4.6

Indexes of Purchasing Value of British Student Grant
(September 1962 = 100)

Year	September	January
1962–63	100	—
1963–64	97	95
1964–65	93.8	93
1965–66	95	93.3
1966–67	91	88.8
1967–68	89.3	88.1
1968–69	88.6	86.7
1969–70	82.3	80.2
1970–71	79.4	77.3
1971–72	81.2	78.9
1972–73	75.1	72.6
1973–74	66.2	63.5
1974–75	79.4	76.2

Source: David H. McKay, "The Political Response to Fiscal Crisis: The Case of Higher Education in Britain and the U. S." (Paper read at the 1975 annual meetings of the American Political Science Association, San Francisco, September 2–5, 1975).

of grants, in the face of accelerating inflation, means that less well-off families now bear more responsibility for actual university expenses.

The New Consensus

These cumulative policy decisions of recent years represent a consensus that has been forged during this period between both major political parties and the civil servants in the DES. For a variety of reasons, these developments have suited all their interests in different ways. The DES has been able to increase its policy-making and controlling capacity. The Conservatives have been able to cut costs in a very expansive social service that had already begun to lose political support in the late 1960s because of student attitudes and behavior, and because of the more important loss of confidence in higher education as an economic panacea for the nation. And the Labour Party has been able to resolve, at least partially, the tension between the egalitarian principle and the more meritocratic concept, which has always been present in their policies for education. During Labour's period of office in the 1960s, despite its commitment to the binary system, the privileged university sector was allowed to expand, as the meritocrats won the struggle for resources. The policy of the 1970s, however, has marked a shift toward the egalitarian or populist principle, as the underprivileged sectors of the system have been favored at the expense of the relatively privileged. [15] For Labour, this shift represents the transference to the arena of higher education of the equalitarian policies and principles it has pursued in the secondary sector during the past decade. Recurrent economic crises, forcing major cuts in public expenditure, have only strengthened the case for a policy of rationalization and redistribution of scarce resources.

But the consistent criticism of these politics by representatives of all the major institutions of higher education, teachers' professional associations, and the National Union of Students indicates the extent to which the consensus on the style and content of policy that has emerged under these pressures is limited to a political elite. Major reservations about current policy developments center on a number of themes. In the first place, higher education policy in the period has been erratic, with frequent shifts in direction occurring, often with little obvious justification. In particular, it has been argued that policy changes, like expansion or contraction of the education sector, have been made in response to changing projections of social and economic need, in periods when such projections "are subject to great uncertainty and [when] they embody many arbitrary assumptions." [16] It may be argued that higher education should respond to long-term goals rather than responding simply to the fluctuation of the marketplace. Also, policy has been internally divisive, as different sectors have been rewarded or restricted at different times and have been placed in competition with each other for resources. It is clear that the development of the polytechnics has been at the expense of the universities.

Underlying this dilemma is the fact that there has been no clear government position on the proper relationship between the mass and elite institutions—the polytechnics and the universities—nor on how the demands for social justice and equality of opportunity may be reconciled with the need to preserve standards of excellence in a period of austerity. The Labour Party, in particular, has remained badly divided on this issue in relation to the binary system. And policy has been increasingly dominated by a search for economy that has proven illusory. Recent evidence suggests that the cost of producing graduates in some polytechnics has become greater than it is in universities. And there is the danger that since the public sector will not receive the resources necessary to fully develop its potential, the effect of the leveling policy will be to lower standards universally across the sector. This fear seems justified in view of the impact that cuts in government expenditure have had upon local-education-authority expenditure in recent years.

Equally important, these trends may in fact reinforce middle-class dominance of higher education. Increased competition for a limited number of places will have the effect of continuing the under-representation of the working classes in higher education. Working-class students have comprised almost half of part-time, or sandwich-course, enrollments in the public sector, but the polytechnics have increasingly sought only full-time students, of which a third have been working class. Service to the working class is further reduced as the polytechnics seek to become more research oriented and less pure teaching. So the percentage of working-class students attending universities declines, and the working-class constituency of the polytechnics declines as they gain universitylike status. In this way, policy leveling may hurt its intended beneficiaries.

NOTES

1. Anthony Sampson, The New Anatomy of Britain (New York: Stein and Day, 1972), p. 157.

2. A. H. Halsey and Martin Trow, The British Academics (London: Faber and Faber, 1971), p. 67.

3. Sampson, op. cit. , p. 168.

4. See R. Layard and F. J. King, "The Impact of Robbins," in Decision-Making in British Education, ed. Gerald Fowler et al. (London: Heinemann, 1973), pp. 227-51.

5. Committee on Higher Education, "Higher Education," Command 2154, (London: Her Majesty's Stationery Office, 1963).

6. David Apelstein, "Roots of the British Crisis," in Student Power, ed. Alexander Cockburn and Robin Blackburn (Baltimore: Penguin Books, 1969), pp. 59-81.

7. See John Pratt and Tyrrell Burgess, The Polytechnics (London: Pitman, 1974).

8. Anthony Crosland, Speech delivered at Wolverhampton Polytechnic, April 27, 1965.

9. Lord Robbins, Speech delivered in the House of Lords, December 1965.

10. Times Higher Educational Supplement (London), April 6, 1973.

11. Times Higher Educational Supplement, December 8, 1972.

12. Times Higher Educational Supplement, May 23, 1975, p. 7.

13. Times Higher Educational Supplement, May 16, 1975, p. 1.

14. David H. McKay, "The Political Response to Fiscal Crisis: The Case of Higher Education in Britain and the U. S. " (Paper read at the annual meetings of the American Political Science Association, San Francisco, September 2-5, 1975).

15. Times Higher Educational Supplement, February 16, 1973.

16. Times Higher Educational Supplement, January 10, 1975.

5

HIGHER EDUCATION:
POLICY LEVELING IN AMERICA

Retrenchment in American higher education is reflected in the disintegration in the 1970s of a de facto national differential-opportunity scheme. Federal government policy traditionally was committed to the decentralized nature of policy making in American education. But the policies were not made randomly. Rather, they fitted into the notion that mass access to higher education is critical, without fundamentally disturbing the status of well-off institutions and citizens. Consequently, differential opportunity was an ingenious way of reconciling the American commitment to equal opportunity with the realities of a socially stratified division of labor, and socially unequal distributions of educational resources and statuses.

During an expansionary period, it was possible to provide quality education in selective, and expensive, private colleges, and in the great public universities, while fostering the government's role in providing the disadvantaged with enormous access to community colleges, proprietary schools, and emerging forms of postsecondary education.[1] No matter that only 17 percent of community college students came from the professional-managerial class, while 72 percent of the students at elite private colleges came from that class. Each level of the system—the academically highly selective institutions of national repute, the moderately selective comprehensive colleges and state universities, and the unselective two-year and four-year institutions—fulfilled the American dream's creed that each person could go to college and that each might succeed. So long as the resources were available to support an expanding differential-opportunity scheme, governmental policy makers could compensate for their relative lack of control as compared with their Western European counterparts. However, recent changes in the social uses of educational policy have combined with structural limitations on policy makers to disrupt the differential-opportunity agenda.

The normal course of educational policy making is largely governed by the realities of obtainable resources and political structure. The fiscal problems are clear enough, given the reduced share of the gross national product allocated to education in the 1970s. For example, both the federal government and the State of New York, a progressive leader in educational policy, allocated fewer uninflated dollars in 1975 than they had in 1970, at a time when the socially created demand for more education had been established among American youth.

The structural problems follow textbook accounts of American federalism and the plurality of power centers. Washington contributes about one-third of all postsecondary funds, with state-local sources accounting for another third of total support. The remainder comes from private sources, chiefly student tuition and foundation contributions. It follows that federal policy makers lack the control over resources that is available to their colleagues in London's Department of Education and Science, and in most Western European education ministries. Moreover, power within the American federal government is widely diffused and intermixed with the numerous social purposes for which support to education has been provided.

The US Office of Education is located within the Department of Health, Education and Welfare, itself a hodgepodge of multiple and ungovernable interests. Federal power over higher education is diffused among 35 agencies, which administer about 400 programs that concern colleges and universities. Congressional responsibility for these programs is spread among 16 US Senate committees and 18 standing committees in the US House of Representatives. Figure 5.1 dramatizes the absence of centralized, national hegemony over American colleges and universities. In addition, Washington's higher education lobby is a melange of sectoral interests, representing everything from two-year schools to the university guild's elite, thereby helping to frustrate efforts to enact a comprehensive national policy.

In this respect, the achievements of the concerned interest groups have not been impressive. The Washington-based education lobby lost the fight to expand funding in the 1970s. They failed in an attempt to commit more federal aid directly to colleges and universities in 1972. And they have still not secured funding for those colleges that enroll federally supported students— the so-called cost-of-education provision of the Education Amendments of 1972. The absence of transcending political movements weakens the position of those who want greater federal commitment to higher and lower education.

The higher education lobby itself reflects the pull of sectoral and local interests. Private giving accounts for about 8 percent of higher education support, and three of every four private dollars go to private colleges and universities. The national university guild,

FIGURE 5.1

Number of Federal Programs Affecting Postsecondary Education by Committee Jurisdiction in the US House of Representatives and Senate

HOUSE \ SENATE	Aeronautical & Space Sciences	Agricultural & Forestry	Appropriations	Armed Services	Banking, Housing & Urban Affairs	Commerce	Finance	Foreign Relations	Government Operations	Interior & Insular Affairs	Judiciary	Labor & Public Welfare	Post Office & Civil Service	Public Works	Veterans' Affairs	District of Columbia	TOTAL HOUSE
Agriculture		14															14
Appropriations			3														3
Armed Services				13													13
Banking & Currency					8												8
District of Columbia																1	1
Education & Labor										3		114					117
International Relations								7									7
Government Operations									1								1
House Administration												4	1				5
Interior & Insular Affairs										12							12
Interstate & Foreign Commerce	1					7	10		2			125		12			157
Judiciary							2	1			11						14
Merchant Marine & Fisheries						3						1					4
Post Office & Civil Service									2				1				3
Public Works	1											1		9			11
Science & Technology	4					1						32					37
Veterans' Affairs															11		11
Ways & Means							8										8
TOTAL SENATE	6	14	3	13	8	11	20	8	5	15	11	277	1	22	11	1	*426

*In addition, the Joint Committee on Atomic Energy has 13 programs under its jurisdiction.

Source: Robert C. Andringa, "The View from the Hill," Change, April 1976. Reprinted with permission from Change, vol. 8, no. 3, © 1976 by Council on Learning, New Rochelle, New York.

defined as 165 major research universities with doctoral programs, enrolls about one-third of all American college students. However, these universities spend 60 percent of all available resources, and are the major beneficiaries of the $3 billion spent by the federal government on research and development (R and D). Indeed, 20 major universities currently receive about half of federal R and D money. One must add the $13.5 billion American corporations spend annually on research and development. More than half of this sum is made up of government subsidies that are not included in federal higher education budgets.

FEDERAL SUPPORT AND HIGHER EDUCATION: THE 1972 LEGISLATION

The history of federal educational policy reveals an intimate link with pressing political goals—for example, the link between the National Defense Education Act of 1958 and the realities of Soviet hegemony; between the landmark elementary-secondary, and higher education legislation of 1965 and the social goals of the Great Society; and between the thrust of the universal-access movement and the Education Amendments of 1972. The tip of this federal iceberg appears most visibly in the 1972 legislation, which directly controls the allocation of about 7 billion federal dollars to higher education. This sum represents about one-fifth of all direct higher education expenditures, and perhaps 10 percent of all knowledge-industry transactions involving colleges and universities. This is the basis of the key political significance of concerted federal action and its indirect influence upon retrenchment policies of the state, local, and private sectors of higher education.

The power base of the federal government in higher education was guaranteed by the 1972 legislation. Toward the end of the 1960s the problems of a declining growth rate, growing economic difficulties, continuing demands to equalize opportunity in higher education, and the limitations of existing federal policies converged in pressing for a federal response. Since existing programs needed reauthorization, in 1972 the stage was set for a new initiative that would determine the federal role in higher education for the crucial decade of the 1970s. The central issue legislators faced was the formula that would be used to allocate federal funds, and in particular, whether funds should be allocated directly in the form of institutional aid to universities and colleges, or as individual support for students.

Both models were already in use and both had their supporters. Aid to students had become a well-established principle in the years since the GI Bill. Institutional aid was also available, but generally only on a categorical basis. But by the beginning of the 1970s the higher education lobby had resolved its internal differences and agreed upon the need for "a broad sustained commitment from the federal government to strengthen the higher education system as a whole,"[2] in the form of institutional aid. It felt current federal programs of student aid were adequate.

Support for the alternative student-aid model stressed the consumption, rather than the production, part of the educational process and favored financial support being made available via the individual student, rather than directly to institutions. In this market model, the greatest benefits to individuals and institutions would be realized by allowing student choice to determine the economic success or failure of institutions through enrollment decisions. The model aimed to rationalize the diverse pattern of educational opportunities by eliminating the weakest institutions and rewarding the better ones, at whatever academic level they operated. Also, support for the individual rather than the institution, it was argued, favored those students most directly in need of support, whereas institutional grants would spread support too thinly and might never reach those lower-income students most in need of support. At the same time, institutional aid might encourage institutions to perform inefficiently by subsidizing their high tuition rates and allowing them to avoid rationalizing their commitments.

The aid-for-students approach, paradoxically, combined the goals of both conservative and more radical interests in higher education at the beginning of the 1970s. Free market economists, for example, favored this model, arguing that students should pay the full cost of their education. The establishment-oriented Carnegie Commission on Higher Education, at the turn of the 1960s, also favored student-based aid, as a way of preserving elite institutions, because it feared too great a federal intrusion into higher education if it financed institutions directly. In 1971 the Newman Commission, which had stressed the limits of government ability to resolve the problem of higher education, similarly favored the student-aid solution. But at the same time, an HEW task force endorsed the student-aid approach precisely because it was believed most likely to produce equality of educational opportunity. Its report argued that "while student aid alone will not correct the problem of inequality of opportunity, studies indicate that college going among the poor is significantly influenced by the amount of student aid; . . . an equal sum spent on institutional aid, by contrast, would have far less effect on the quality of opportunity."[3] As observed by the Carnegie Council on Policy Studies in Higher Education, quite unlike the debate during the growth period of the 1960s, "when the needs were seen as complementary, in 1971 and 1972 'student aid' vs. 'institutional aid' became the focal point of a legislative struggle that assumed high symbolic significance."[4]

The Education Amendments of 1972 resolved the debate. The preference of the White House, HEW, and of Congress was for the market-oriented student-aid model. The higher education lobby's demands for institutional aid received hardly any support, in principle or in fact. The legislation also confirmed the major reorientation of federal policy by stressing the need to achieve equality of opportunity in higher education through the provision of funds for low- and low-middle-income-group students. In this respect, the legislation was a paradox, for in the words of one observer, "it almost seemed an anomaly coming from a conservative Republican administration. The program was cast in the mold of 1960's liberalism in the sense that it put first priority on aiding the poor."[5]

However, the package appealed to the different interests concerned for a variety of reasons. For the Nixon administration, the program was compatible with its general preference for eliminating big government and social service bureaucracies, and for placing cash directly in the hands of those who actually needed it. For many in HEW and the Office of Management and Budget (OMB), student aid was regarded as far superior to institutional aid, which was regarded to be financially uncontrollable. And for many in Congress, support for the needy, rather than for universities, seemed a more electorally attractive stance. Thus the legislation meant that the future of federal support for higher education would be a drift away from direct institutional aid and a growth in support for the individual student. Indeed, in the late 1970s, it is clear that "general support for institutions as it was posed in the 1972 debates is no longer a live issue."[6]

The unifying consensus was built around support for differential opportunity. Reformers, such as the Carnegie Council and Newman Commission spokesmen, advocated student choice and the availability of centers of academic excellence and expanding urban community colleges. Congressional liberals supported a Basic Educational Opportunity Grant Program, and conservatives could rest assured that institutions such as Stanford and Dartmouth would never be penetrated by a government-sponsored underclass. The Washington higher education lobby lost the battle for primary funding of colleges and universities in 1972, so-called institutional aid. They correctly saw that the student-choice idea merely repeated the experience of categoric federal grant support by substituting one straitjacket for another. The burden of providing universal access for ill-prepared students was shifted to the states, localities, and colleges. Moreover, discerning educators saw that a conservative market and pricing mechanism was at the heart of the differential-opportunity policy and the federal commitment in 1972:

Those economists and planners, inside the government and elsewhere, who favor such higher levels of tuition at public colleges, more emphasis on student aid for the poor, and long term loans for everyone else have generally opposed institutional aid. Some planners want a market model in which students pay much more and "decide" which college to support. An emphasis on federal and state student aid and student choice can sometimes be a subtle means of raising charges for almost all students. [7]

The 1972 legislation established the Basic Equal Opportunity Grant Program, which entitled all eligible and qualified students to federal support, minus the amount that their families could be expected to contribute toward their college education. Eligibility was based on a family income ceiling, originally $10,000, and qualification applied to all accredited postsecondary institutions, regardless of academic selectivity. These guidelines have applied to packages of student aid, federal and state, establishing a minimum-welfare policy—student support above $2,900 has been rare. By 1976, Secretary Matthews of HEW formalized the existing reality that federal policy is to provide a floor for student support. He did not reiterate the obvious consequence, namely, that unselective, low-income students were being channeled into unselective and low-cost, open-access institutions.

The 1972 amendments also provided that any direct aid to colleges would largely be determined by federal student-aid policy. In fact, 45 percent of any institutional support was to be allocated per enrolled BEOG student, and 45 percent was to be distributed per recipient of other forms of federal student support (work-study payments, supplementary educational opportunity grants). This cost-of-education grant to colleges and universities has never been funded. The 1972 amendments also spawned new agencies: a network of 1,202 commissions to solidify state-federal efforts; a National Institute of Education, charged with the support and execution of basic educational research; a Fund for the Improvement of Post-Secondary Education; and supportive provisions for the cause of affirmative action that affected every college and university in America.

The 1972 legislation thus represented "a major step towards a policy of federal aid to higher education that would be designed primarily to encourage equality of opportunity."[8] It was designed to encourage free student choice of institutions and fields of study; to encourage diversity and preserve institutional autonomy by emphasizing aid to students rather than to institutions; to aid both public and private institutions; and to ensure greater equality of opportunity by guaranteeing that funds were available to regions and institutions with large numbers of low-income students.

Individuals, rather than institutions, were to be favored. Egalitarian, rather than elitist, principles dominated the allocation of federal largesse. There was no systematic direct support for institutions. These trends were accompanied by a growing federal preoccupation with the internal organization and the practices of universities, in contrast with the federal government's previous concern with the output of higher education in terms of manpower. The trends were confirmed by the 1976 Higher Education Act, which changed some of the details but left the main features of federal policy intact.

Among the major beneficiaries of the 1972 legislation were government bureaucrats. The expansion of student aid elevated the power of the Office of Education. New domains of influence were created by establishing the National Institute of Education and the postsecondary education fund. Since nothing in the 1972 amendments affected the market mechanism for distributing high-quality, expensive education, Conservatives correctly saw reform as a way to preserve the de facto stratification of American higher education. In the case of Washington's affirmative-action program, radical chic and Nixonian policy coincided in the expansion of two agencies charged with securing compliance by American colleges and universities. The staffs of both the Civil Rights Division and the Equal Employment Opportunity Commission were largely recruited from campus radicals of the 1960s. And, in fact, these were among the few domestic agencies whose budgets were greatly enlarged during the Nixon presidency. Consequently, the cumulative impact of the 1972 amendments worked against the autonomy of American colleges and universities. Indeed, the antiinstitutional bias was a major cement in the multiple alliances that developed. Central bureaucratic power was expanded under a tripartite banner focusing on liberty, equality, and efficiency. Student aid channeled low-income-group, unselective students into the unselective, cheap, open-access sector. [9]

Between 1967 and 1972 the college population had doubled. Previously, between the passage of the GI Bill in 1945 and the 1965 Higher Education Act, it had taken two decades for the college population to double. The 1972 amendments were intended to cope with this social explosion by providing universal, postsecondary access for racial minorities and low-income students. [10] The percentage of entering freshmen from families below the national median-income level increased from 32 to 42 percent between 1967 and 1974. This gain was made at the expense of students from the highest income quartile, whose contribution to the college ranks declined 8 percent between 1967 and 1974. Perhaps the most significant fact of the period was the academic transformation of postsecondary students. Between 1962 and

1974 alone, mean college board scores fell 34 points on the verbal section, and 22 in mathematics. The percentage of college attenders who had been in the top quarter of their high school class declined from 80 to 54 percent between 1960 and 1970. The enrollment in public two-year community colleges doubled between 1965 and 1975, going from 12 to 24 percent of all higher education enrollments, based on full-time equivalents. Another 9 percent were in the least selective private four-year and two-year colleges. By the most rudimentary index of admissions selectivity, one-third of the American college population was in open-access institutions maintaining minimal academic standards. [11]

The result was a differential-opportunity system without the enormous governmental investment required to succeed under the best of economic and educational conditions. Indeed, the probable results of the 1972 Education Amendments were already available in California, where 68 percent of the state's high school graduates entered college. [12] Under the California plan, any high school graduate who could profit from instruction was eligible to attend a community college. Half of California's postsecondary enrollment was in the community colleges; yet only 46 percent continued beyond their freshman year, and only 23 percent of the community college entrants obtained degrees. Indeed, the attrition rate in the open-access tier of California public higher education rose from 43 percent in 1958 to 64 percent in 1972. This revolving-door phenomenon of open-access, postsecondary education is reinforced by regional comparisons. Between 1960 and 1972, of all the regions, the Pacific and Mountain regions—in effect, the most equalitarian sections of the country—had the largest proportion of college entrants, but the lowest proportions of students continuing beyond their first year, those going beyond their second year, and baccalaureate graduates. Significantly, other regions of the country provided four years of college or more to a larger proportion of the total college-age-population than did either California, or the Pacific and Mountain regions. The social costs of universal access, much less the problem of retrenchment, were never contemplated by the architects of the 1972 legislation. [13]

Retrenchment Policy: A Mix of Factors

American retrenchment policy reflects this mix of federal, state, local, and market factors. The major tendencies are explicit federal education acts; ripple effects among American state systems; and a de facto pricing system by which the costs of quality, public higher education are shifted to the consumer. Consider, first, the impact of the 1972 legislation. The new distributive formula, allocating a shrinking pie, maximized student aid at the expense of direct aid to colleges and universities. The critical point is found in the consequential social costs and benefits of this policy during retrenchment. Between 1972 and 1976, federal higher education support actually declined while demand increased slightly.

As recently as 1965, student aid accounted for only 17 percent of Washington's contribution, while institutional support amounted to 25 percent of federal aid to higher education. A decade later, students received 56 percent, and colleges only 9 percent, of total higher education funds. By 1976, the federal government was distributing $5.50 of student aid for every $1.00 of institutional support. The dramatic changes in federal allocations to students and their colleges are plotted in Figure 5.2.[14]

The expansion of federal student aid, including veterans' and social security benefits, is very significant. Because student aid grew at the expense of institutional support, American colleges and universities were hard pressed to provide necessary educational services. This problem was compounded by the welfare benefit contours of emerging federal policy. In practice, federal student support, most visibly the Basic Educational Opportunity Grant Program, channeled unselective students into open-access institutions. The ceiling on eligibility and per-student support meant that colleges had incentives to enroll these students, but other sources were needed to pay increasing educational costs. The history of categoric research grants, in which the availability of federal funds determined the scope of programs, was repeated with the same outcome, namely, that universities were eventually stuck with the bills. Moreover, the 1972 policy placed new strains on hard-pressed states, cities, and private foundations.[15]

The rise of student aid was matched by the demise of direct aid to colleges and universities at every turn. In 1972, the Nixon administration vetoed a bill providing $1 billion for construction, graduate fellowships, community service programs, and college libraries. In the same year, the BEOG program was funded with $1 billion. In 1975, President Ford vetoed a bill providing institutional aid for an almost identical list of programs and facilities, while reorganizing student aid to stretch scarce dollars. Federal student-aid policy gave support to the new wave of postsecondary students. Between 1965 and 1975, these new students were low academic achievers from families with low or modest incomes, and the major institutional expansion to accommodate them occurred in the community college, open-enrollment, and unselective private college programs. Eighty-five percent of open-access students—those attending unselective colleges—are currently eligible for BEOG, compared with 44 percent attending middle-range comprehensive colleges, and 23 percent in the undergraduate colleges of the national university guild.

FIGURE 5.2

Federal Support to Colleges, Students, Research, 1961–77

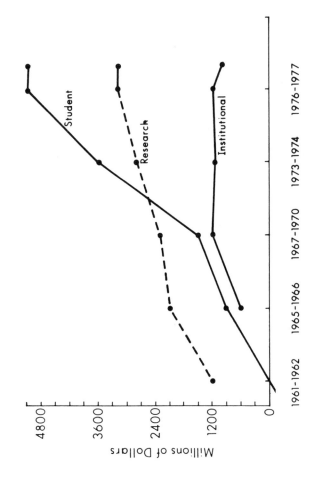

Source: Carnegie Council on Policy Studies in Higher Education, The Federal Role in Post-Secondary Education (San Francisco: Jossey-Bass, 1975). Used with permission. Copyright © 1975 by The Carnegie Foundation for the Advancement of Teaching and Jossey-Bass, Inc. Publishers.

The major social cost of federal policy is paid by middle-class students, whose only visible characteristic is high academic potential, and by the public universities and comprehensive colleges. For example, comprehensive colleges—defined as liberal arts institutions with some graduate programs below the doctoral level—enroll one-third of the student population, and spend about 28 percent of all funds available to higher education. However, community college students are twice as likely to receive federal support than are students in more academically selective institutions.

The spiraling costs of college education, and the federal bounty for enrolling high-risk and high-cost students, affect most American colleges. One of the characteristics of university budgets is the limitation on transferring funds from one purpose to another. The categoric aid nature of federal aid is duplicated in many states, testimony to the high price of consensus among diverse special-interest groups.

Since 1972, partisan and institutional conflicts have centered on the size of the higher education budget and the extent of the predominant student-aid share. Democratic-controlled House and Senate committees have supported larger budgets and more generous student-aid packages than have Republican presidents. Nevertheless, when a House education subcommittee considered proposals to shift federal funds from students to colleges, and to award some student aid on the basis of academic merit, not entitlement, there was a stony silence at the hearings.

The fiscal problems of retrenchment are sharpened only if there are social expectations about the distribution of higher learning. Federal retrenchment policy has its counterparts in the states. Bearing in mind that the problems of state universities in the Northeast are more acutely affected by the cycle of economic recession and recovery than those in less industrialized states, we looked at the public higher education policies in four northeastern states (New York, Connecticut, Massachusetts, and New Jersey) in order to gauge the cumulative impact of recent state policy upon the progressive ideal. [16]

The progressive ideal holds that students, regardless of social or economic station, can pursue higher education, at public expense, to the limits of their capabilities. The bastions of this concept have been the better public universities and comprehensive colleges. Social policies of the 1960s provided for the education of a meritocratic elite, an elite that countered the historical dominance of exclusive and expensive private colleges. The giant California and State University of New York (SUNY) systems provided quality education obtainable without the interplay of wealth, power, and culture that defines the establishment and the social function of institutions such as Williams or Princeton.

In the 1970s the northeastern public higher education systems have changed, with the use of policy leveling—that is, the offering of cheaper education at a higher price. This process particularly diminishes the progressivism of their best public universities, thereby reestablishing the distance between private elite and public mass education. In actuality, the equalitarian amendments of 1972 contribute to more stratification within American higher education.

Between 1972 and 1975, selected private colleges of the Northeast increased their tuition and fees an average of 15 percent. A year's residence at an excellent private college now costs at least $6,000. In effect, this pricing mechanism excludes many middle- and lower-middle-income students of high academic achievement. In the public sector of higher education, Connecticut, New York, New Jersey, and Massachusetts operate three-tier systems, stratified in terms of resources, degree offerings, prestige, tuition, and faculty salary and professional status. There is a university subsystem at the top; a four-year state college subsystem, usually consisting of former teachers' training institutes, in the middle; and a two-year community college subsystem at the bottom. Over the last three years, tuition and fees have increased about 20 percent, on the average, across the university tier—university centers, in the State University of New York's nomenclature—of the four states.

The public university tier in these states is taking on a pronounced upper-middle-class flavor. In this tier, between 1971 and 1975, the proportion of students with family incomes exceeding $25,000 increased by 17 percent in Connecticut, 19 percent in New Jersey, 13 percent in Massachusetts, and 11 percent in New York. These better-off students comprised only 8 percent of the University of Connecticut student body in 1971, and 25 percent of the total in 1975.

Data from the American Council on Education confirm the widening social gap between highly selective and unselective public institutions. Figure 5.3 compares meritocratic universities—public institutions with highly selective students—with mass colleges—four-year public colleges with very unselective students.[17] The meritocratic schools were even more merit oriented in 1975 than they were in 1973, in terms of the percentage of entering freshmen with B+-or-better high school grades. Thus the gap between them and the mass colleges has increased in terms of enrollment of academically bright students. Moreover, the difference in the proportion of better-off students, in terms of father's education and family income, has widened between the meritocratic and mass public institutions.

In another sense, cutting the public universities down to size makes them more like two- and four-year public colleges. The switch of resources from liberal arts to vocational areas within universities is based on a misguided notion of efficiency and on the belief that busi-

FIGURE 5.3

The Social Gap between Selective and Unselective Institutions, 1973-76

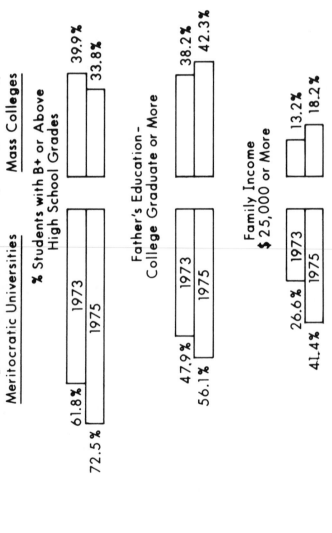

Source: Alexander W. Astin and Associates, The American Freshman: National Norms (Washington, D. C.: American Council on Education, 1973 and 1975).

ness and engineering students are more likely to get jobs than are humanities and social science majors. Contrary to the notion of Marxist scholars, the actual fit between the educational and occupational sectors is quite loose in the United States. Lacking the labor market mechanisms common in Europe, there is little assurance that redeploying college resources in vocational programs will yield more jobs. Indeed, the experience of the community college movement illustrates the problem. Community colleges have wavered between purely vocational programs that lead to modest, but assured, employment gains, and a comprehensive academic program with higher dropout rates and lower employment payoffs. The vocational route confirms the class-stratified nature of American higher education, while the comprehensive form sustains the illusion of equal opportunity in the context of graded academic achievement. The community college declines further in status to the degree that it becomes more vocational. This is the German practice in a stratified, but vocationally productive, higher education system. But it conflicts with the American equalitarian norm; hence, the emphasis on comprehensive academics that seem more equal in status with programs of other institutions.

The leveling of public universities is likely to both decrease their number of blue-collar students and to channel the rest into more vocational programs. The community college experience suggests this trend: blue-collar students comprise 35 percent of those going into vocational programs, but only 5 percent of the university-bound group. Black community college students comprise 14 percent of the vocational group and only 5 percent of the academic-college group. The expansion of the community college, open-access level increased the differentiation between it and the high-status public universities. Leveling these public universities will have comparable consequences vis-à-vis the private colleges and universities. California has 80 percent of its postsecondary students in community colleges (the national figure is 33 percent). However, it is exceedingly difficult for students to transfer to Berkeley, Santa Barbara, or any of the other selective university campuses. As public universities become more like two- and four-year public colleges, the probabilities of high-quality public universities—alternatives to high-quality private, elite institutions—are diminished. Students at elite private universities come from families where 85 percent of their fathers have some college education. At the other end of the higher education pyramid, only 34 percent of community college students have fathers with comparable educational attainment. [18] More striking is the fact that social class differences between public universities and other public institutions exceed the differences between public universities and all private universities. Using data reviewed by Karabel, for example, one finds the social class index, that is, occupation, parental education, and family income, was 83 (the highest index would be 100) for students at private universities, 62 for those at public universities, and 34 for those at other public postsecondary institutions. Moreover, social differentiation on each item (education, occupation, and income) was greater between public universities and other public institutions than between public and private universities.

The significance of the social differences between state universities and other institutions in public higher education is that redistributing funds or students to the community and four-year colleges levels the public sector while increasing the social and academic distance between quality state universities and the private universities. Indeed, this is true whether the redistribution is accomplished through funds, lower-quality students (under the open-access and affirmative-action programs), or tuition increases pricing out bright, modest-income students. The lowering of academic standards at public universities has the same effect since community college students are more likely to resemble noncollege students, in academic aptitude, than university students. Indeed, policy leveling has become explicit policy. For example, in 1978 the New York Board of Regents recommended that access to public higher education be unlimited, but that one-third of the doctoral programs at the university centers be phased out. Although rejected by Governor Carey, the proposal had serious implications.

The policy impact of higher education is influenced by the availability of fiscal resources to different kinds of students at various types of institutions. Figure 5.4 looks at the sources of student financial aid. Students at highly selective schools have more access to private resources than do students at unselective schools. By contrast, students at the mass public colleges have somewhat more access to packages of federal aid than do students at meritocratic public universities. The distribution of state scholarships and grants favors the better students at the meritocratic public universities.

Rather than labor the point that quality public universities are responding to the market and pricing out less well-off students, we can illustrate the declining quality of public higher education. We have looked at the distribution of budget cuts within each tier of the four state systems we studied. Unlike the British case, state and community colleges do not benefit at the university's expense. The four states vary in their degree of centralized administration—New York has a strongly centralized system, while New Jersey and Connecticut have more fragmented decision-making processes. In no case is there the unitary power of the British DES operating unchallenged in higher education policy formation.

The deterioration of high-quality public universities is more subtle that what we have described above. In reviewing policy decisions in all four states, we found the consistent retrenchment pattern involves

FIGURE 5.4

Sources of Student Support, 1975

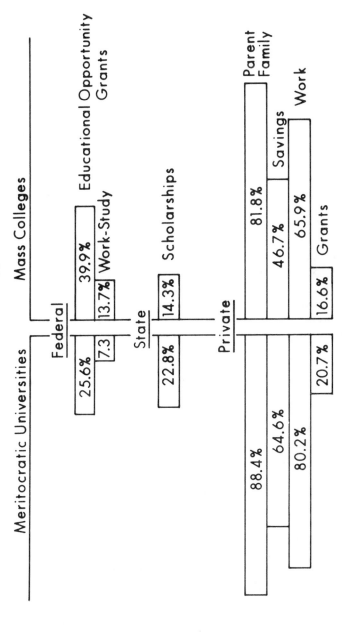

Source: Alexander W. Astin and Associates, The American Freshman: National Norms (Washington, D. C. : American Council on Education, 1973 and 1975).

the quality of intellectual life. Some of this can be neatly quantified—for example, increasing ratios of students to staff, declining library purchases, reduced equipment budgets. However, the inner life of a university is not determined by the per-student book holdings in the library. There were also reductions in graduate programs, particularly in the humanities and applied social sciences; a curtailment of innovative programs begun in the 1960s, ranging from black studies to honors programs; a reduction of travel privileges and telephone usage. In sum, there was a curtailment of those substantive and stylistic amenities that support a healthy climate of learning and scholarship. Consequently, the pricing system offers students less quality at higher cost, while increasing the opportunity costs of the socially average students. In dollar terms, expensive items on the public university's menu are curtailed or passed on to student consumers who can afford them. Yet, quality and expense are relative terms. The most salient observation one comes away with after reviewing budgetary policies at SUNY, for example, or in Albany, or at Rutgers University is the unwillingness, or inability, of state government to play the patron role required to sustain the intangible benefits of art, culture, and higher learning.

The federal pattern is reinforced in the expansion of bureaucracies charged with coordinating and rationalizing state higher education systems. Legislative efforts to secure greater efficiency, reorganization, and control have been made in all four states. Ultimately, the mentality of the cost accountant, that "a student is a student is a student," and "a school is a school is a school," becomes pervasive. It is in this profound sense that policy leveling erodes distinctive qualities of academic excellence, ability, or distinction.

Federal policy since 1972 has concentrated on providing minimum benefits in postsecondary education. The loss of institutional support resulted in the funding of social welfare clients at the bottom of the public higher education systems. Faced with budgetary strains, state governments have cut their commitment to higher education, with resulting policy rationalizations driving costly social goods out of the public domain. Rationalization results in both the passing along of the costs of quality public higher education to the consumer, and the reduction of many indexes of quality. Consequently, the gap between superior public and private universities widens, with profound implications for the social distribution of culture, opportunity, and prestige.

The American retrenchment pattern, then, is a mixture of minimum social welfare benefits and the increased role of the private market in determining the distribution of higher education and its presumed advantages. The problem is articulated in proposals made to congressional committees in 1975, which called for federal higher education support to students on a sliding scale that took into account both fiscal need and the academic selectivity of the college to which the student is admitted. A companion proposal would greatly increase direct aid to colleges and universities, with priorities given to two types of institutions: the highly selective, and those with low tuitions and fees. Clearly, both proposals would aid public universities and comprehensive colleges who provide opportunity for the bright, upwardly mobile students from nonmonied backgrounds. These efforts have failed to produce any concrete results. Consequently, the outlook is for the continued deterioration of public higher education, the merging of public universities and community colleges, and the re-emergence of socially stratified opportunities for those in the elite private and mass public sectors.

In both Britain and the United States, the growth in the scale, cost, and economic significance of higher education in the past decade has led governments to become increasingly involved in its planning and financing. Relations between the two sectors have become increasingly formal, and less flexible, as government has inevitably involved itself in the private as well as the public life of institutions of higher education. And as the costs of support have escalated, economic considerations have become more dominant in the minds of decision makers. The dilemma for both government and higher education is that, while economic constraints are an inevitable dimension of policy, they are not necessarily the most appropriate criterion that can be employed in determining long-term social policy; for example, great weight may be attached to the needs and demands of both clients and professional providers of higher education. The experience of the higher education sectors in both countries in recent years has highlighted these dilemmas.

The trend in policy has been a search for cheaper solutions to demands for mass access to higher education. The trend in policy making has been the gradual centralization of government decision making at the expense of other interest groups. The result has been the creation of rigidities and contradictions in policy. The tensions between the imperatives of elite and mass demands have been exacerbated rather than resolved. In the United States the 1972 Education Amendments reinforced open access to postsecondary institutions. Several linked policies were pursued to advance toward the goal of universal mass education. These involved the creation of institutions that were cheaper than the traditional universities, to accommodate the new clientele; the lowering of occupational expectations of graduates; the upgrading of existing disciplines and qualifications; a guaranteed educational minimum with special protection for the underprivileged; and the growth of a comprehensive planning and coordinating agency. American federal policy has already moved markedly in this direction. Many of these features are found in recent British government policies also.

This rationalization has occurred in a period of severe financial stress, which gives rise to concern that the long-term aim of the policies is to restrict, rather than develop, the system of higher education. This raises two broad questions: what should be the direction of future policy, and how can it best be formulated? The two considerations are interrelated. A new strategy is needed to reconcile elite and mass demands in higher education and, in particular, to define the optimal role of the universities. Through the 1960s the universities were favored; and other American public postsecondary institutions were relatively neglected. In the 1970s the situation has been reversed. The experience with the British binary system in this period has been similar. And both policies have grave social, economic, and intellectual costs. Social justice might demand fair treatment for the disadvantaged and community colleges, but this should not imply that university interests should be jeopardized. The point has particular force in regard to the US state universities that combine quality with merited access. Yet, economic constraints have created this situation. Despite government advisers' reassurances to the contrary, the current improvement of the mass public colleges has been at the expense of the elite universities. Resources have been transferred from one sector to the other. And despite claims of efficiency and equality, higher education is becoming more stratified, price conscious, and impoverished.

Equally important, the introduction of simple cost criteria has had distorting effects upon policy. It has led to the favoring of the mass public colleges and the leveling of higher education in general, on the grounds that the colleges are cheaper. But this policy has merely served to defeat its own objective by making the overall product more expensive. And at the same time, it has led to the deterioration of the physical and intellectual capital that was developed in the universities in their halcyon days. In this respect both political parties and governments have refused to realize that to balance the equally legitimate interests of both public spheres requires that adequate funding be committed to both sides. To develop one part at the expense of the other is misguided, in the long term proving both costly and socially unjust. It will force up overall costs in the public sector, and reaffirm the minority, and therefore elite, status of the private sector. It will make university education available only to the well off. If expenditures on American state comprehensive universities are reduced, as in present governmental policy, the position is worsened. At worst, if adequate resources cannot be produced, decision makers should develop more sophisticated criteria than current costs to evaluate long-term effects and implications of policies.

A sound policy would need to integrate the costs and diverse demands in a coherent institutional framework. The problems of planning long-term measures toward mass education, while maintaining standards of excellence in an era of financial austerity, are acute. Such a model, incorporating a variety of institutions in a flexible system aspiring to a variety of goals, might seem appropriate, particularly if it meant that policy and planning were based on long-term considerations. A flexible series of institutions that allowed mobility between the various levels would also help eliminate the problem of defining precisely the function and status of the various parts of the system, particularly as common agreement upon the definitions does not appear possible anyway.

Such a system could well meet the demands for a cheaper form of mass education that would not necessarily sacrifice standards of academic excellence. The universities could be protected from the often unreasonable criticism they have endured during the past five years, and long-term plans for the expansion of higher education, which might well be necessary by the 1980s, could be made. But the system would depend upon each sector receiving financial resources. The system should also be free from a too-restrictive central direction that limits diversity and opportunity. Coordination has become essential in an age of financial stringency, in order to maximize the use of scarce resources. But the danger is that as coordination becomes "more regulatory and more bureaucratic, it is likely to standardize the institutions under its surveillance instead of encouraging invention and a variety of means of attaining educational purposes and designated missions."[19]

Such a policy also has implications for the appropriate model that should be adopted for social policy making. A system that has become too closed and dependent upon simple criteria, such as costs or current demand, is bound to distort the needs and interests of a particular social sector. In higher education we have seen that the tendency has been to commit both sins—overcentralizing decision making and making simple cost criteria dominant. The two are intimately related. Pressures to cut expenditure have compelled governments to centralize power and rationalize provisions, both of which are rarely successful as the basis of policy. For example, higher education policies, which have been based upon projection of future demand, apart from being questionable in principle, have inevitably been flawed. Cost calculations can cut the intellectual heart out of a university.

Yet, we must anticipate continued fiscal restrictions and the loss of confidence in higher education's promise among political elites. Then, policy choices will no longer be vertical at different tiers of formal systems. Retrenchment will proceed across whole programs and academic disciplines. The hope is that sensitive decision makers will be capable of qualitative judgments about social knowledge. Higher education policy involves judgments about intangibles. For example, what are the influences of liberal arts over a lifetime, and what is the impact of scholarly research upon society? The universities will fare better in the hands of sophisticated patrons and politicians, than in the application of bureaucratic mediocrity that fears nothing so much as the creative and the innovative.

NOTES

1. See Carnegie Foundation for the Advancement of Teaching, More Than Survival: Prospects for Higher Education in a Period of Uncertainty (San Francisco: Jossey-Bass, 1975); Carnegie Commission on Higher Education, Higher Education: Who Pays? (New York: Mc-Graw-Hill, 1973); Carnegie Council on Policy Studies in Higher Education, The Federal Role in Post-Secondary Education (San Francisco: Jossey-Bass, 1975); Edgar Litt, "The Counter-Reformation in Higher Education Policy," American Behavioral Scientist, (Spring 1974): 531-54.

2. Lawrence E. Gladieux and Thomas R. Wolanin, Congress and the Colleges (Lexington, Mass.: D.C. Heath, 1976), p. 45.

3. Ibid., p. 53.

4. Carnegie Foundation, op. cit., p. 112.

5. Gladieux and Wolanin, op. cit., p. 69.

6. Ibid., p. 247.

7. John Malin, "The Cost of Education Controversy," Change, June 1973; US House of Representatives, Committee on Education and Labor, Hearings on Education Amendments of 1972, 92d Cong., 1st sess., 1971.

8. W. L. Hanses and R. J. Lampman, "Basic Opportunity Grants for Higher Education," Challenge 17, no. 5 (1974): 46-51; Edgar Litt, "Successes and Failures of Equal Opportunity Programs in the United States," Proceedings of the Society for Research Into Higher Education (London), 1974, pp. 69-90.

9. Hanses and Lampman, op. cit., pp. 46-51; Litt, op. cit., pp. 69-90.

10. College Entrance Examination Board, Toward Equal Opportunity for Higher Education: Report on the Panel on Financing Low-Income and Minority Students in Higher Education (Princeton, N.J.: CEEB, 1973); R. W. Hartman, "Higher Education Subsidies: An Analysis of Selected Programs in Current Legislation," in Joint Economic Committee, US Congress, The Economics of Federal Subsidy Programs: Part 4, Higher Education and Manpower Subsidies (Washington, D.C.: US Government Printing Office, 1972).

11. Based on data supplied by Center for Institutional Research, University of Connecticut.

12. Werner Hirsch, "Open Enrollment: Quo Vadis?" in Universal Higher Education: Costs, Benefits, Options, ed. Logan Wilson and Olive Mills (Washington, D. C.: American Council on Education, 1972), pp. 223-44.

13. Based on data supplied by Center for Institutional Research, University of Connecticut.

14. Federal aid data are based on Office of Education appropriations, 1965-75; and on Issues of Change, The Chronicle of Higher Education, The Congressional Quarterly Weekly Report; Carnegie Foundation, op. cit.; Carnegie Council, op. cit.; Carnegie Commission, op. cit.

15. On federal retrenchment, see Barry Blechman et al., Setting National Priorities, The 1976 Budget (Washington: Brookings Institution, 1976), pp. 48-65.

16. Data on the states were supplied by Louis Rabinow, Connecticut Commissioner of higher education; Kevin Harrington, majority leader, Massachusetts State Senate; and Edward Hollander, higher education chancellor, New York State.

17. Selectivity is based on median college board scores. The differences between meritocratic public universities and mass public colleges are from Alexander W. Astin and Associates, The American Freshman: National Norms (Washington, D. C.: American Council on Education, 1973 and 1975).

18. See Jerome Karabel, "Community Colleges and Social Stratification: Submerged Class Conflict in American Higher Education," Harvard Educational Review 42 (November 1972): 521-62.

19. T. R. McConnell, "Coordinating Higher Education," Higher Education Review 8, no. 1 (1975): 56.

PART III

SCHOOL POLICY:
THE REFORM
OF EDUCATION

INTRODUCTION

During the 1960s social changes in education preoccupied both Britain and America at the elementary and secondary school levels. Indeed, the reform of education is a major preoccupation of American life. Concerns about racial segregation, local control, political interference, and equality of opportunity pervade US discussion of the subject. No single volume can hope to do justice to this immense political fabric. Rather, we have concentrated upon one critical and controversial part of it, the role that federal and state governments have played in recent years in trying to redistribute resources so that more equitable schools might exist. Whether or not equality of funding produces equality of academic achievement is a subject of immense, and unresolved, debate. The political point, however, is that communities, states, and national agencies act as if these resource allocations matter.

The British school situation is different from the American for a number of reasons. The ranges of educational expenditures per pupil, and corresponding differences in quality between the various local education authorities, are much smaller than those existing among or between American states. Also, the British and European problem has been to modernize hierarchical educational structures, created for the perpetuation of a governing elite. By contrast, the comprehensive high school, and majority graduation of each age group, are customary in the United States. It was only in 1972 that the British Labour Party raised the compulsory school-leaving age to 16. By the age of 18, only 41 percent of British children are in school, compared with 93 percent in the United States. This is despite the fact that Britain spends a greater portion of its gross national product (6.5 percent in 1972) on education than does the United States.

As early as 1959, the Crowther report found that an upper-middle-class child was three times as likely to continue schooling beyond 15 than was a working-class child with equal intelligence. And in 1968, only one in 25 students in the ordinary schools (so-called secondary modern schools) continued in school after reaching 17. By contrast, one in two students in the high-quality schools (public, direct-grant, and maintained grammar schools), advanced to more schooling after 17. The stranglehold maintained by the upper social classes, quality schools, and their supporters on British life was enormous.

The introduction of the comprehensive schools to alleviate this impact of the social past upon one's social future has been significant. Between 1968 and 1978, the proportion of comprehensive schools in the British state school system grew from 19 percent to 75 percent. They have effectively replaced the old secondary modern and technical schools that consigned working-class youth to unequal educational and social opportunities. The British comprehensive-school movement is less dramatic than that of Sweden, where 95 percent of students are in comprehensive schools, but it is far ahead of West Germany, where less than 20 percent of schools are comprehensive.

However, the parallel with the American case, where the Elementary and Secondary Education Act produced mild reform, is striking. As in America, British comprehensive schools are usually tracked—that is, they have different programs. Indeed, the variety of actual comprehensive and academic arrangements is enormous, ranging from the case where the local grammar school still takes the best pupils, to highly experimental plans where mixed-ability groups and unitary tracking are used. In European terms, the British are, again, midway between the Germans, with their hierarchical schooling predicated on the elite gymnasium, and the Swedes, who have merged vocational and academic programs into a single system, where any program can lead to higher education.

The continuing diminution of elite institutions in British education presents a second-order problem familiar to Americans. In the United States, white suburbs and racially mixed inner cities commonly have educational systems that enormously influence life chances, in opposite directions. The fact that both the city and suburban systems are under public auspices means little to those familiar with the differences in physical plant, teacher quality, and college attendance records that characterize city and suburban schools.

The British, having preoccupied themselves for 20 years with institutional reform and the creation of a more equalitarian school structure, now have to face similar problems. Even if genuine nonselective comprehensive-school systems can be attained, the disparity in quality created by neighborhood school systems will remain. Neighborhoods obviously vary in the resources they can bring to the school system, and in this sense, a system of nonselective neighborhood-based schools obviously exaggerates the significance of such disparities in the community. Also, many comprehensive schools are merely fusions of underprivileged secondary modern schools and remain relatively underprivileged in terms of the quality of their students, staff, and resources available to them. Simply renaming an institution does not change its essential characteristics, especially when many other schools represented mergers of successful grammar schools and retained many of the advantages of those institutions.

In their anxiety to create a nonselective system, decision makers have not seriously addressed the problems of areal inequality among LEAs. These problems will be even more significant because the traditional route of educational and social mobility for a minority consisting of talented working-class children—the state grammar and direct-grant schools—has been progressively eliminated by the comprehensive-school movement. Despite the uncertainty about the relative significance of class and family background, as opposed to the impact of formal schooling upon children's educational attainment, the American experience suggests that the relative segregation of working-class and middle-class children in nonselective neighborhood-based comprehensive schools, without the possibility of transfer that once existed in the selective system, may have the adverse and unintended consequence of discriminating against working-class children.

The middle-class comprehensive schools may thus become dominant in the same way that the best suburban high schools are paramount in America. The irony is that, despite the political heat generated by the social and fiscal aspects of educational reform in both countries, the relative inequality of the poor may not have been significantly diminished. Today the comprehensive schools dominate the state educational sector. Nevertheless, the growth and success of the comprehensive schools—which depend on how well the costs of reform match up with the benefits—remains as much a matter of controversy in Britain as in America.

In the future, administrators in Britain will have to confront some of the unintended consequences of the institutional reform they have assiduously pursued for two decades in their search for greater equality of opportunity. In particular, they will have to pay much more attention to the internal processes and practices of schools, rather than to external organizational characteristics alone, in order to maximize equality of educational opportunity. The danger of penalizing intellectually able working-class children by confining them to inferior comprehensive schools may not be as practically or morally significant as was the case under the tripartite school system (grammar, technical, and secondary modern schools). But the problems need to be addressed, and strategies found that will minimize resource disparities and maximize opportunities. For example, positive discrimination in favor of relatively deprived neighborhoods and their schools may not be the only way to proceed, but local authorities might be encouraged to explore such possibilities, and the differential allocation of local resources, most seriously. Similarly, the virtues and vices of tracking in comprehensive schools will need to be more systematically addressed if equality of opportunity is to be achieved for all pupils.

There is evidence that the central government has become more concerned with such educational issues in recent years; witness the DES's projected survey of attainment in comprehensive schools. But this concern may have to be expanded. The increase in leadership power at the center means that the government needs to be even more flexible and sensitive to these issues than was the case when a more decentralized pattern prevailed. This is not to question the desirability or legitimacy of recent policy changes, but merely to point out the obvious problems that flow from them. Guaranteeing equality of opportunity for underprivileged groups may in fact be a task which is finally beyond the scope of government; but once having initiated it, the government has a responsibility to address, as clearly as possible, the problems it raises. The assumption of greater central power makes the responsibility even more onerous.

6

COMPREHENSIVE-EDUCATION MOVEMENT IN BRITAIN

The major policy changes that have taken place in higher education in Britain since the early 1960s have been paralleled by developments in the secondary education sector, as the national government has sought to increase equality of opportunity. At the beginning of the 1960s Britain had a stratified, selective pattern of secondary schools that provided clearly differentiated educational opportunities for the different social classes. A decade later, a series of policy initiatives by two Labour administrations had substantially changed that pattern and laid the basis of a system of nonselective comprehensive schools that at least had the potential to eliminate inequalities of class opportunity in education.

Also during this period, the central government and the DES have become much more willing to exert increased control over the traditional providers of secondary education, the LEAs, as they have done over the institutions of higher education. In 1964-70, a Labour government, anxious to initiate reform with as little political controversy as possible and to avoid antagonizing the local authorities, relied upon persuasion rather than legislation to achieve national goals. But since 1974, the Labour government and the DES have become much more willing to compel the LEAs to implement national policies and to use sanctions, if necessary, against those who are unwilling to do so.

FACING INEQUALITY

The pressures to reform secondary education in Britain during the 1950s and 1960s stemmed from a growing professional and public realization that the major reforms of the school system introduced by the 1944 Education Act, while offering a formally more egalitarian system of secondary education, had not achieved their goal of increasing the real educational opportunities of disadvantaged, working-class children. [1] That legislation had made free secondary education available to all children from all social classes for the first time. But rather than creating common secondary schools on the American high school pattern, it had set up a selective tripartite system consisting of academic grammar schools, technical schools, and nonselective secondary modern schools, which provided qualitatively different kinds of education for allegedly different clientele. The grammar schools remained the most prestigious, best-equipped, and most educationally desirable part of the sector, preparing pupils for entry into the professional classes, often via the universities. Differential financing of the different kinds of schools helped to maintain educational and social distinctions. And although entry to the grammar schools was based upon performance in public examinations, a bias continued to operate in favor of middle-class children.

The reforms of 1944 had produced a marginal reduction in inequality. Whereas before 1944 less than 10 percent of working-class children gained entry to the grammar schools, in the 1950s this proportion had risen to 20 percent. But it still compared badly with the 70 percent of middle-class children who gained access to the grammar schools. Class disadvantage had been reduced somewhat, but a middle-class child still had four times as great a chance of getting a grammar school education as the child of a skilled worker and nine times the chance of an unskilled worker's child. Entry to the higher reaches of English education was also directly correlated with social class. One in four middle-class grammar school entrants went on to a university; only one in 15 grammar school entrants from unskilled workers' homes got that far. [2] In the 1950s, therefore, Britain, like many other European countries, still faced the problem of developing educational policies that would give the children of all social classes at least a formal guarantee of an equal secondary education.

The solution that became increasingly popular throughout the 1950s and 1960s was the creation of a nonstratified system of nonselective comprehensive schools to replace the tripartite system. But between 1951 and 1964 the Conservative Party held power nationally and broadly resisted pressure for change, generally refusing permission to Labour-controlled local educational authorities to introduce any general school reforms that would eliminate the elite, selective grammar schools. Nevertheless, in response to pressures from a number of Labour LEAs, Conservative ministers did sanction very limited experiments with comprehensive schools during this period; and when the Conservatives lost control of government after 13 years in power, there were a small number (183) of comprehensive schools in operation throughout England and Wales. But as the Labour Party took office in 1964, there remained an almost universal selective system of secondary education.

By that time, Labour, which had progressively shifted its attention from purer class issues toward more status-oriented problems of British society throughout the 1950s, had become the most important advocate of comprehensive education in Britain. [3] That position had not been reached without a degree of internal conflict, however. The party had originally supported the selective system that had emerged from the 1944 Education Act on the grounds that it would benefit many working-class children by giving them access to the prestigious grammar schools from which they had been previously excluded. The two decades since then had been spent in resolving the dispute between those sections of the party who were prepared to tolerate the tripartite system, and the reformers, who insisted on pressing for comprehensive schools. The party had formally committed itself to comprehensive schools in the early 1950s, but some lingering doubts remained after that among both the leadership and mass membership of the party. [4] Consequently, during this period, little attention was paid to planning the practical aspects of school reform.

Labour's Strategy, 1964-70

When Labour assumed office in 1964, it had made a general commitment to the principle of comprehensive education, but had not resolved a number of critical strategic issues concerned with the implementation of its program. The most important was the general strategy a Labour government should employ in implementing a national reform program, and, specifically, whether it should attempt to persuade local authorities to implement reform by issuing a conventional departmental circular, or whether it should use mandatory legislation to enforce change. The second strategic issue to be decided was the extent of resources that could be made available to encourage local compliance, and the nature of the sanctions that should be employed in the face of potential resistance to a central government initiative, either by the local education authorities, or by the wide variety of selective-entry church schools, direct-grant schools, and wholly independent schools that provided places for state pupils.

The choice of strategies was affected by a number of structural features of the relationship between the central government and local governments in Britain, which differ markedly from those in the United States. The first was the relatively large powers the national government can generally exercise over local authorities; and, in particular, the authority the DES has as a policy-making and controlling agency in relation to local education authorities, in contrast to powers traditionally exercised by its US counterpart, the Office of

Education. By the mid-1960s, the DES had developed a series of elaborate controls over both the material and academic aspects of local school systems, which, reinforced by the fact that the central government contributed 65 percent toward local authority expenditure, gave it considerable political leverage over subnational units. [5] By contrast, the US Office of Education, which contributes only 8 percent of local school district expenditures, and which had traditionally been confined to the collection and dissemination of educational statistics, had little significant power to control and evaluate the performance of local school districts.

In Britain, also, the capacity of local authorities to resist the formal and informal controls exercised by the central government is weakened by a number of other factors: that there are relatively few education authorities, that they have limited financial independence, and that they are integrated directly into the machinery of local government. Central government authority is also increased by the existence of relatively disciplined local party systems, which generally pursue the educational goals of their respective national parties. All of these factors tend to reduce local variations in education policy and increase the potential success of central reform initiatives. [6] The need for central pressure to enforce policy is correspondingly reduced. By contrast, the 16,000 school districts in the United States stand as autonomous units outside the normal local government's structure, exercising great discretion over their taxation rates and expenditure policies. Also, being nonpartisan, they have no organized relationships with the national parties that could serve as a reference point for local policies. They have a correspondingly greater ability to resist central government policy initiatives, which, as we shall see, clearly affected the success of federal reform policies of the mid-1960s.

These structural differences help account for the fact that, on assuming office in 1964, the Labour government adopted a permissive, rather than a mandatory, legislative strategy for reform and did indeed have some measure of success with it. It relied upon a circular, 10/65, which simply requested LEAs to submit their reorganization plans to DES within 12 months, rather than introducing legislation that would enforce it. There were some good reasons for adopting this strategy at this time. The government wished to encourage the incipient trend to comprehensive schools apparent at the local level, without breaking the traditional consensus of education politics in Britain, and without alienating conservative opinion by pursuing a too-aggressive policy against grammar schools. And Labour calculated significant change could be realized without legislation. But, although it was not widely realized at the time, the circular had a number of serious weaknesses, partly stemming from Labour's failure to plan the details of reform when it was the opposition party. There was, for example, no legal pressure upon LEAs to submit schemes. There were no clear sanctions available to employ against recalcitrant authorities. And there were no new sources of finance specifically made available to implement the changes locally.

Nevertheless, such was the dominance of the DES in English education that this permissive strategy received a positive initial response from the LEAs. In the first year after the circular was issued, 50 percent of LEAs submitted plans that were implemented or approved. This led, in the period from 1967 to 1969, to the annual addition of some 200-250 comprehensive schools, as many as had been created in the 20 years from 1944 to 1964. However, after the initial submission of genuine plans by the poorer, smaller, and predominantly Labour-controlled LEAs, the submission rate began to drop as Conservative-controlled LEAs began to engage in delaying tactics, such as extended negotiations, the submission of clearly unacceptable plans, or, in the case of a sizable number of recalcitrants, the refusal to submit any plan at all. By mid-1968, 31 LEAs were classified as "uncooperative" because they had either not submitted plans or had submitted plans that were rejected. If plans were returned for being patently noncomprehensive, the LEAs simply continued their selective systems. Those which did not submit at all realized that the government did not possess the legal power of final sanction until it supplemented the permissive portions of the 1944 act with mandatory powers contained in new legislation.

By 1969 it was clear that the original impetus of the reform movement at the local level had been exhausted, and that the government would soon have to deal with the hard-core minority of LEAs who were refusing to cooperate fully in its policy of adding comprehensive schools. And in that year the government, rather reluctantly, introduced legislation to reorganize the schools. But loss of office in 1970 prevented that legislation from becoming law.

Labour's Achievement

The achievement of the Labour government in implementing its program in the period 1964-70 may be evaluated differently, according to the stringency of the criteria applied. The most critical interpretation would emphasize that only 10 percent of secondary pupils were in wholly nonselective school systems when Labour left office. Labour's critics have suggested a variety of reasons, both of a long-term and short-term nature, to explain the apparent slowness in achieving changes. Some have stressed the ideological ambiguity in the party's program for change in education. Others have stressed a relative lack of interest in secondary education generally in the party. On ocassion, it is blamed for its failures as the opposition party, namely, the failure to produce in the 1950s and early 1960s a concrete strategy for implementing its general goals. More often, it is criticized for its failures in office, especially the failure to introduce legislation earlier. [7]

Nevertheless, significant gains were achieved under Labour, as can be seen in Table 6.1. The rapid growth in comprehensive schools after 1964 indicates the degree of success Labour's program enjoyed. When it left office in 1970, the number of comprehensives had grown from 184 in 1964 to 1,256. The number of grammar schools had been reduced from a peak of 1,298 in 1964 to 1,038. The nature and timing of the planning process also meant that the continued growth in comprehensive schools in the years immediately following Labour's departure from office was, in many cases, the product of LEA planning that had taken place under the auspices of Labour's Circular 10/65. In June 1970, for example, 115 local authorities had plans for the whole or greater part of their areas actually implemented or approved for implementation by the Labour government. It was these gains that explain the fact that, despite Conservative control of the DES, the number of comprehensive schools grew from 1,520 to 2,137 between 1971 and 1974, and the percentage of children in them continued to grow, from 37.6 percent in 1971 to 62 percent in 1974.

Some of this change was accounted for by Conservative-controlled LEAs, but the vast bulk of the school reorganization took place in Labour authorities, as indeed it had between 1964 and 1970. For example, of the 115 LEAs who had approval for reorganization in 1970, only 17 had had uninterrupted Conservative control since 1966. The great majority of the rest had been Labour controlled for the entire period or significant parts of it. Of the 17 LEAs who had partial approval for their plans, only two were Conservative; the remainder were Labour. Sixteen had had their plans turned down by the Labour-controlled DES; all had had Conservative administrations for the major part of the period between 1966 and 1970, when LEA planning for reorganization had been taking place. Five LEAs submitted their plans so late that the Labour government had not had time to evaluate them before they left office; all of these were Conservative. Of the ten who simply did not reply to Circular 10/65, seven had had uninterrupted Conservative control; the others had had either no clear party system or a brief period of Labour control. Clearly, Labour had made a major impact upon the pattern of secondary schools in Britain.

On assuming office in 1970, the Conservative government, therefore, faced a fait accompli, which it was substantially unable to reverse. So much political controversy had been generated at the national and local levels that the government regarded it as impossible

TABLE 6.1

Growth of Comprehensive Education in England and Wales, 1952-75

Year (at January 1)	Total Number of Grammar Schools	Total Number of Comprehensive Schools	Percentage of Secondary Students in Comprehensive Schools
1952	1,189	9	—
1953	1,184	11	—
1954	1,181	13	—
1955	1,180	16	—
1956	1,193	31	—
1957	1,206	43	—
1958	1,241	86	—
1959	1,252	111	—
1960	1,268	130	—
1961	1,284	138	—
1962	1,287	152	—
1963	1,295	175	—
1964	1,298	195	—
1965	1,285	262	8.6
1966	1,273	387	10.2
1967	1,236	508	14.1
1968	1,155	748	20.9
1969	1,098	962	26.3
1970	1,038	1256	32.0
1971	970	1520	37.6
1972	893	1777	43.4
1973	819	2137	48.2
1974	675	2677	62.0
1975	566	3064	69.7
1976	477	3387	75.6

Note: Dash indicates information not available.
Source: Statistics of Education: Schools, Department of Education and Science, London H.M.S.O., relevent years.

to mandate another restructuring of LEA systems, which had only recently undergone reorganization. Its primary goal became the preservation of the status quo, and of the enormously heterogeneous pattern of educational provision that then prevailed. Thus, Circular 10/70, which the Conservatives used to immediately replace Circular 10/65, essentially removed the obligation upon LEAs to reorganize, and left that decision to the discretion of the local unit. More broadly, the government's strategy was to eliminate the financial incentives for LEAs to reorganize; to create ambiguity about its own preferences and thus restrict LEA capacity to make long-term plans; and to more readily accept LEA schemes that would lead to the demise of nonselective schools, as opposed to schemes that threatened the prestigious grammar schools. Thus, while the Labour government had tended to give total approval for the majority of the LEA schemes they received, the Conservative government usually gave only partial approval. Of the 24 LEAs that were allowed to reorganize between 1970 and 1974, 20 of them were given only partial approval. In most cases, approval was given for the demise of secondary modern schools, and withheld in the sections of the schemes that affected grammar schools. And throughout the period, as LEAs increasingly and inevitably confronted the remaining selective schools, the government became increasingly critical of their submissions and unwilling to approve them. In 1970–71, for example, the DES rejected 20 LEA proposals to change schools status; in 1971–72 and in 1972–73, 220 proposals were rejected. So, while unable to reverse the basic trend toward reorganization, the Conservative government was able to dilute and delay that process.

The Assertion of Power—1974

When Labour returned to office for a second time during the decade, therefore, the problems it faced in implementing change were very different from those of 1964. Then, their major task was to persuade the majority of LEAs to begin the process of reorganization. By 1974, that first phase had been completed. Many LEAs had responded to Labour's original policy and had implemented reform. Labour's problems in 1974 were created, first, by the small minority of LEAs that had refused to make any efforts to reorganize their school systems; and, second, by the much larger number who were, in principle, willing to reorganize but, for a variety of reasons, had not advanced very far in that direction.

Many of these had only partially reorganized or had only received partial approval for implementation of reorganization, either because they were basically unwilling to change or because of the genuine difficulties they experienced in devising satisfactory schemes that would include all the selective grammar schools and church schools. This second category was rather more important since Conservative control of the DES had not stopped the main thrust toward secondary school reorganization, but had diverted it by encouraging LEAs to retain some element of selection or selective schools within their reorganized systems.

Thus in 1974 the absolute number of comprehensive schools was quite large: There were 2,677 comprehensive schools in England and Wales, representing 49 percent of all secondary schools and admitting 62 percent of all pupils in maintained secondary schools. But these aggregate figures conceal the extensive variation that occurred within specific local authorities. When Labour took office, 32 LEAs had not submitted plans for reorganization; 71 LEAs had DES approval for partial reorganization only; and of the 60 who already had received approval, 15 still had substantial numbers of unreorganized voluntary selective schools. [8] The position was aggravated by impending reorganization of local government, which, in April 1974, led to the mergers of LEAs and a reduction in the number of LEAs outside London, from 143 to 83, and a reduction nationally, of 164 LEAs to 104. In many cases, this structural reorganization involved the fusion of Labour-controlled LEAs with reorganized secondary systems, and the fusion of Conservative-controlled LEAs with unreorganized secondary sectors. Developments in many of these LEAs remained uncertain.

The main issue Labour faced was the strategy it should adopt in relation to the LEAs that had not reorganized their schools, and, specifically, whether it would continue to use a permissive strategy as in 1964-70, or whether it would attempt to impose national goals directly upon local authorities by introducing legislation requiring school reorganization. Initially, the Labour government took the first option, although immediately upon taking office, the new Labour minister of education withdrew the Conservative Circular 10/70, and invited all the newly created LEAs that were assuming power on April 1 to resubmit to the department any existing proposals that had been submitted by the old LEAs but had been rejected by the Conservative minister. [9]

In April, the Labour government introduced a departmental circular, rather than legislation, to help complete reorganization of LEAs. Circular 10/74 requested all local authorities who were operating a partially selective school system to submit plans for the introduction or completion of reorganization by the end of 1974. As of March 31, the termination date for the old LEAs, this involved 76 LEAs who had approval for partial reorganization only, and 15 who had no DES approval at all.

Labour was not prepared to use legislation at this time for a number of reasons. In the first place, the close election of 1974 meant that the Labour government was essentially a minority government, dependent upon the support of a variety of minor parties and unwilling to risk fracturing a coalition with controversial legislation. But also, as in 1964-70, Labour's hope was that the DES could use its authority over LEAs to persuade the bulk of them to conform, and that the minority of recalcitrant authorities would eventually undermine their own position by alienating public opinion with their dogmatic refusal to cooperate. At the same time, it was felt that the DES would have sufficient difficulty in processing and evaluating the LEA schemes that would be submitted, and should not have to worry about the position in a few delinquent authorities. The DES also hoped that the creation of the new local authorities, which would result in mergers of some of the recalcitrant LEAs with some who already had comprehensive-school systems, might produce a local resolution of the problem without the need for too much central direction. The Labour education minister, however, confirmed his desire to press ahead with voluntary reorganization by approving seven LEA school reorganization schemes in his first month of office.

However, Labour did adopt a more aggressive approach on two issues that it had virtually neglected in its first period of office but that, over the years, had complicated enormously the reorganization process. The first was the reluctance of church authorities to reorganize their secondary schools, which, in some large cities like London, Birmingham, and Liverpool, had seriously undermined local comprehensive-school schemes. Circular 10/75 was used to indicate to those schools that they could expect major cuts in public financial support if they refused to cooperate with their LEAs in the future and to be integrated into completely comprehensive systems.

In March 1975, the government also took action on one other problematic kind of school, the direct-grant schools. The existence of these 175 selective schools, who were basically anomalously independent, but received significant public financial support in the form of grants and fees, had complicated the government's problems in forcing LEAs to eliminate all selective practices within their jurisdiction. In Labour's first period of office, despite the obvious affront by these schools in regard to the principle of unselective education it was trying to enforce in the public sector, the Labour government had been unwilling to force a change in their status and they were allowed to survive intact. But in 1975 Labour's policy shifted and the minister announced that in the future, state grants to the direct-grant schools would be phased out. It gave those schools the choice of merging completely with the maintained sector, or of becoming wholly private institutions without direct public support, or of actually closing their doors if they were unable to survive economically. This policy decision considerably simplified the potential problems of local reorganization by curtailing the capacity of Conservative LEAs to undermine local comprehensive-school schemes by purchasing places in the selective schools for their most academically capable pupils and thereby siphoning them out of the public sector. It also demonstrated the growing willingness of the DES to confront the difficult and controversial practical problems inherent in the principle of comprehensive education.

Nevertheless, by January 1975, the target date set by Circular 10/74, it was clear that, although the majority of authorities would conform at least with the letter of the minister's request, a hard-core minority would never accede without mandatory legislation, and that many others had seriously limited schemes for reorganization. Indeed, a national survey that year documented in detail the precise limitations of many local schemes. [10]

It revealed that, nationally, 70 percent of all pupils were in comprehensive schools and less than 10 percent were in selective grammar schools, but that local variations again seriously qualified the overall pattern. Only 20 of the 104 LEAs in September 1975 had totally non-selective comprehensive-school systems, and three of those still bought places at direct-grant or independent schools. A further 20 had a wholly comprehensive maintained sector, but had major problems in integrating the voluntary school sector that attracted pupils from the state comprehensive schools and sustained some form of local selection. Another 25 LEAs had had plans approved for complete reorganization but could not implement them for a further five years. The remaining 39 LEAs had set no specific date for completing reorganization and had made only a rather suspect commitment, saying they would reorganize "sometime" in the distant future. And seven LEAs were still insisting that they would "never" have a comprehensive-school system. Another 34 LEAs who claimed to have a system that was partly comprehensive retained over 25 percent of their pupils in selective schools. The extent of the continuation of selective schemes and schools and the extent of local variation are shown in Table 6.2.

Mandatory Legislation

This situation forced the government to reassess its policy, and by the autumn it was clear that it had changed its previous position and was prepared to use central authority to impose changes upon the local authorities. In August, for the first time, the education minister provided £25 million in funds, specifically earmarked to aid the reorganization process. In September, a letter was circulated to all the local authority associations and national bodies responsible for voluntary schools, outlining proposals to enforce local reorganization and

TABLE 6.2

Number of Local Education Authorities with Various Percentages of Children in Comprehensive Schools, 1975

Extent of Local Reorganization	Percentage of Pupils in Comprehensive Schools	Number of LEAs in each Category
0		1
1–10		3
11–20		7
21–30		2
31–40		5
41–50		5
51–60		7
61–70		9
71–80		14
81–90		18
91–99		13
100		20

Source: Times Educational Supplement, March 21, 1975.

to acquire powers giving the minister the authority to review all LEA arrangements for taking pupil places at nonmaintained schools.

And in November, legislation designed to eliminate selective schools and force the seven recalcitrant LEAs to reorganize on comprehensive lines was introduced in Parliament. It proposed that all LEAs should observe the principle of comprehensive education, "that all education should be provided in schools in which pupils were admitted without reference to ability or aptitude," and gave the minister powers to require LEAs to submit a comprehensive-school scheme within a specified date. If LEA proposals were unsatisfactory, the minister had the power to reject them and call for new proposals. No final date was set for the process of completion of reorganization, but the minister assured Parliament that he would need to be convinced that LEAs were going ahead "at reasonable speed and diligence," and that he would expect voluntary schools to submit realistic proposals that they could afford to implement.

The legislation took over a year to get through both houses of Parliament as the Conservative Party in both the Commons and the Lords opposed the bill in some detail. The Conservative opposition consistently attempted to introduce amendments that would delay the reform until more resources were available, or until more was known about the educational impact of reorganization, and that would retain the principle of internal selection, to protect the status of particular disciplines like mathematics. But none of these types of amendments was accepted, as Labour pressed the bill through in the Commons. For a period of time, the Conservatives in the Lords threatened to destroy the legislation in the 1976 session, as they had done with other Labour government nationalization legislation, but after a heated internal debate and a split vote, resistance in the Lords was dropped, and the act became law in November 1976. Only three amendments had been accepted by Labour, the most significant of which permitted the use of selection procedures by LEAs, not to produce schools with pupils of above-average ability, but rather to prevent the emergence of schools with a majority of below-average pupils.

The introduction of legislation marked a new and more active phase in governmental and DES efforts to force local authorities to reorganize their school systems. With the new legislative powers at her disposal, the new Labour minister of education acted quickly to enforce the policy. LEAs were immediately advised that, although the government would not force unsatisfactory schemes upon them, it would "expect authorities and voluntary bodies to reply responsibly with the law." Within a few weeks, the minister wrote to the recalcitrant LEAs who had never submitted proposals for reorganization, requiring them to submit their plans to go comprehensive within six months. Two circulars also were produced. One drew the attention of all LEAs to the minister's intention to implement reorganization rapidly, and urged them to cooperate. The second heavily emphasized the new powers that the minister had for reviewing and terminating any arrangements that LEAs had made to purchase places in independent schools for intellectually gifted children, and stressed the minister's willingness to use her powers if those arrangements undermined local comprehensive schemes.

A 1977 survey revealed the extent of this problem and the degree to which Conservative LEAs had employed this technique to maintain selectivity in the secondary sector. [11] The survey showed that 46 of 104 LEAs had attempted to evade the implications of comprehensive education by purchasing significant numbers of places in private schools, with these places constituting around 2-4 percent of their total provision in many cases, and significantly more in some others, at a cost in each case of over half a million pounds. Many of those 46 LEAs had not progressed very far with reorganization; and of those who had made progress, with over 90 percent of their pupils in comprehensive schools, 17 of them still took a large number of places in private schools. Over three-quarters of those 46 LEAs were controlled by the Conservative Party.

The minister, confirming the urgency she attached to achieving reform later in the year, initiated action against a group of 26 LEAs that had previously had plans for reorganization approved by the DES but had set no specific time for their completion. Six of them were required to submit plans, within six months, to reorganize their existing secondary schools; 12 were required to reorganize some part of their area where selective schools remained, again within the six months; and the remaining eight were required to produce plans, within six months, phasing out voluntary schools where admissions procedures were still conducted on a selective basis.

CONCLUSION

The process of reorganization is continuing, but 12 years after its original initiative in 1965, Labour had persuaded LEAs to place 75 percent of their secondary school pupils in comprehensive schools. Many critics have argued that if Labour had introduced legislation between 1964 and 1970, more could have been achieved more rapidly. However accurate that view, it is clear that the introduction of legislation in 1975, and its vigorous enforcement since then, will speed up the process of reform.

Recent events confirm that, in this area as in many others, the government and the DES have increased their resolve to assert their authority over the local education authorities and shown their willingness to adopt detailed strategies to enforce the implementation of national programs.

The government adopted this more activist position despite the legal reversal it suffered in one case. In 1975 the Conservative Party, which took power in the Thameside LEA, successfully challenged the order of the minister of education that the LEA should proceed with the comprehensive scheme that had been introduced by its Labour predecessor. In a historic judgment in June 1976, the Law Lords confirmed that the LEA had not been "acting unreasonably," as the minister had claimed, in refusing to reorganize its school system, and that the minister did not have the authority to force it to do so under the powers of the 1944 Education Act, as he had also claimed. As a result, the minister withdrew the order, and the LEA was able to reintroduce a selective secondary school system. Despite the controversy generated by the affair, it did not set a precedent, nor did it significantly deter the DES in its future relations with local authorities. And, of course, after the passage of Labour's legislation later in the year, the government's authority to enforce reorganization was wholly confirmed.

Despite the reality of the educational alliance in policy making, the central government has always played a significant role in the organization and provision of education in Britain. Its capacity to do so has been enhanced by a variety of factors: the extent of legal constraints it can impose upon local government expenditure; the existence of a dominant party system integrated at the national and local government levels; and the relative lack of legitimacy that is accorded to local community resistance to nationally prescribed policies. But in recent years, the central administration has played an even more dominant part in elaboration of policies and practices, as our case study of school reorganization has made clear. At what point the costs of centralization are perceived to outweigh the benefits remains at issue. But if central government dominance is reduced in the future, it is likely to occur as a result of the DES's own calculations of the matrix of advantage, rather than of those of its partners in the educational alliance.

NOTES

1. See J. Floud, A. H. Halsey, and F. Martin, Social Class and Educational Opportunity (London: Heinemann, 1957).

2. Alan Little and John Westergaard, "The Trend of Class Differentials," British Journal of Sociology 15 (1964): 302.

3. See C. A. R. Crosland, The Future of Socialism (London: Jonathan Cape, 1956).

4. See Michael Parkinson, The Labour Party and the Organization of Secondary Education (London: Routledge, Kegan Paul, 1970).

5. See Maurice Kogan, Educational Policy Making (London: Allen & Unwin, 1975).

6. See Noel T. Boaden and Robert A. Alford, "Sources of Diversity in English Local Government Decisions," Public Administration 47 (1969): 203-4.

7. See Caroline Benn and Brian Simon, Halfway There: A Report on the Comprehensives (London: McGraw-Hill, 1972).

8. Times Educational Supplement (London), March 15, 1974.

9. Ibid.

10. Times Educational Supplement, May 21, 1975.

11. Times Educational Supplement, February 18, 1977.

7

THE REFORM OF SCHOOL FINANCE
IN AMERICA

The differences between British and American education structures are clear enough: centralized versus decentralized funding tied to local property taxes in the United States; the clear primacy of the British Department of Education and Science, contrasted with the amorphous role of the Office of Education in Washington; the British reform of local government, leaving the DES with only 100 or so local education authorities, compared with the innumerable centers of education policy in America—cities, towns, counties, states, and special school districts.

Given this multivaried context, we shall deal with one major theme in American education, namely, the equalizing of educational resources and opportunities. We begin with the consideration of federal aid to education in the United States. Then we take up the course of efforts to equalize school funding among and within the states. And we conclude this chapter with an evaluation of the successes and limitations of these remedial efforts. By focusing our inquiry in this manner, we hope to approximate most nearly the context of policy decisions involved in the British comprehensive-education movement dealt with in the previous chapter.

THE IMPACT OF NATIONAL AID TO EDUCATION

Writing more than a decade ago, Robert Bendiner observed:

Proposed legislation to aid the schools has been beaten over and over again not because the nation's schools were ever shown to be in admirable or even satisfactory shape, but because of wholly extraneous considerations like race and religion, or secondary ones like a vague fear of Federal control and simple-minded penny pinching. [1]

Federal aid to education has existed since Bendiner's study, but the "extraneous" factors he studied have continued to have a significant impact upon the course of elementary and secondary school funding. A series of social pressures, originating in the civil rights movement of the 1960s, carried forth in the Great Society war on poverty, and sustained by the burden of state-local school taxes in the 1970s, has expanded the federal role in education. Table 7.1 highlights the growth of federal aid: over the course of 20 years, Washington's school support has grown from a half billion dollars to $4.5 billion, and the per-

TABLE 7.1

Contributions to Local Education Expense by Level of Government, 1957-74

| School Year | Percent of School Revenue Derived From: | | |
	Federal Sources	State Sources	Local and Other Sources
1957-58	4.0%	39.4%	56.6%
1958-59	3.6	39.5	56.9
1959-60	4.4	39.1	56.5
1960-61	3.8	39.8	56.4
1961-62	4.3	38.7	56.9
1962-63	3.6	39.3	57.1
1963-64	4.4	39.3	56.4
1964-65	3.8	39.7	56.5
1965-66	7.9	39.1	53.0
1966-67	7.9	39.1	53.0
1967-68	8.8	38.5	52.7
1968-69	7.4	40.0	52.6
1969-70	8.0	39.9	52.1
1970-71	8.4	39.4	52.1
1971-72	8.9	38.3	52.8
1972-73	7.9	40.6	51.5
1973-74	8.2	42.6	49.2
1974-75	7.8	43.6	48.6

Source: Categorical Grants: Their Role and·Design, Advisory Commission on Intergovernmental Relations (Washington, D.C.: US Government Printing Office, 1976).

centage of total school funding provided by federal sources has expanded from 4 to 8 percent.

From approximately $2.5 million in 1919-20, the amount of federal aid grew to $3.3 billion in 1971-72. Major federal enactments providing monies for schools include the National Defense Education Act of 1958, which authorized funds to improve the availability and quality of courses in science, mathematics, and foreign languages. It was enacted the year after the Soviet Union had launched Sputnik I, and reflected a national desire to compete with Russia in the space race. It was with the passage of the 1965 Elementary and Secondary Education Act (ESEA) that the contemporary era of federal aid to education began. In effect, ESEA was the Johnson administration's educational component of the war on poverty. The deep-seated belief that the schools could be mobilized to eradicate the culture of poverty is illustrated in then Commissioner of Education Francis Keppel's words in support of the ESEA:

> Archimedes . . . told us many centuries ago: "Give me a lever long enough and a fulcrum strong enough and I can move the world." Today, at last we have the prospect of a lever long enough and supported strongly enough to do something for our children of poverty. [2]

The key section of the ESEA was Title I, which was to provide educational programs for the culturally deprived. Indeed, Title I received 80 percent of the $1.25 billion initially appropriated, and has been the major source of federal aid to education since 1965. Between 1965 and 1975, a total of $6.7 billion was spent under the ESEA, approximately $1.7 billion per year. Despite this impressive figure, the core politics of the ESEA have involved a constant battle to obtain and distribute scarce funds, when it came to per-pupil support in constant dollars.

From the outset, the politics of coalition building dictated that ESEA funds go to almost every school district in America. Spread over 45 million students, this meant that the 1965 ESEA provided only $40 per pupil. Subsequent developments restrained the impact of Title I and the ESEA, so that today less than 10 percent of school district funds come from all federal sources in 90 percent of the cases. The fruits of decentralized political power in the American system are clear in these data: the per-child Title I funds available between 1966 and 1973 decreased from $210 to $173, even though appropriations, themselves considerably below congressional authorizations, increased from $5.6 billion to $7.9 billion during the same period. These realities mitigated the federal emphasis in favor of low-income children and school districts. Indeed, between 1960 and 1965, before the ESEA was enacted, other federal-aid-to-education programs increased the portion of funding going to children of low-income families from 10 to 26 percent. [3] And, of course, the education of low-income children was at the heart of the ESEA and its key Title I proviso.

The political pattern of the ESEA since its inception consists of renewed efforts to promote equality by helping poorer children and school districts; and then the dashing of expectations by underfunding and executive obstruction, resulting in an intensified struggle for limited resources and power made available to states and localities by the federal government. Regarding the scale of federal funding of Title I, a House of Representatives committee offers this summary: "Equal educational opportunity cannot possibly be achieved by providing only approximately 175 additional dollars a year for each Title I student, which has been the pattern of the program since its inception."[4] The ESEA was to come before the House and Senate for funding and amendments every four years, and by 1973, the second time the ESEA had come up for reconsideration, only $7.8 billion, of the $16.8 billion that had been appropriated, had been spent under Title I. The cold reality, even after subsequent congressional action to vitiate executive impounding of authorized funds, is that, during the last decade, federal aid to education, limited enough by European standards, has been supported at the rate of only 36 percent of the original appropriation.

Bendiner's "extraneous" issues of federal control and support to parochial schools were initially coped with by the Johnson administration's funding equation: $A/2 \times B = P$. As described by Joel Spring, the political formula that initiated the ESEA was as follows:

> Within this formula, A represented a state's average expenditure per pupil and B represented the number of poor children in a school district. In its final legislative form the level of poverty was set at a family income of $2,000. It was felt this could be done without raising the problem of church-state relations because of a Supreme Court ruling in 1947 that the busing of parochial students was aid to the pupils and not to the Catholic Church. When the church-state issue was raised in legislative hearings, the problem was resolved under the child benefit theory. Added to the legislation was a provision that title to all library resources and instructional materials would be vested in a public agency. In turn these materials were to be lent to teachers and pupils in any public or private educational agency approved by the state. What this meant was that this aid would go directly to the teachers and children in parochial schools and not to the schools. [5]

In 1966, national average per-child expenditures replaced individual state expenditure levels as the basis for alloting Title I monies. This change favored the poorer, rural southern states that were a key element in the supporting congressional coalition. For example, Mississippi's share of Title I funds increased from $23.5 million (1967) to $44.8 million (1968). The congressional coalition was further aided by a 1973 directive that the Office of Education could directly serve parochial schools and create separate programs for them. Over time, the limits of poverty eligibility and supportive Office of Education staff were expanded in support of the program. In actual fact, ESEA funding was becoming a shrinking pie to its supporters. For example, between 1971 and 1974 a 2 percent gain in aggregate funding was wiped out by a 10 percent rise in educational costs. The politics of coalition building involved constant congressional-executive battles, not only about funding levels, but about the shape of the program. The congressional view of categoric, constituency-bound aid was countered by presidential initiatives in favor of consolidation proposals that enhanced the accountability of ESEA expenditures. Reflecting on a bloc-grant proposal of the Ford administration in 1975, the lobbyist for the American Association of School Administrators observed: "I've been here for nine years and they've been talking about bloc grants the whole time."[6]

These cumulative frustrations came to a head in 1974. A new poverty formula, the Orshansky index, was offered as a substitute for the AFDC (Aid to Families with Dependent Children) welfare index used in the original ESEA bill. The Orshansky index was based on three factors: size of family, rural-urban domicile, and cost-of-living differential. Consequently, in 1974 the allocation of Title I funds would range from $1,632 for a farm family of one to $5,820 for an urban family of eight. The core issue was political, not technical, centering on the potential impact of the Orshansky index on large cities and the durability of the congressional coalition that had sustained the ESEA against strong opposition. Proponents of the Orshansky poverty index argued that the AFDC formula was inadequate because there were many ineligible people on welfare rolls, and because the states had varying welfare policies and payment levels. They also claimed that the new measure did not discriminate against cities. In fact, New York City, with 6 percent of the nation's poor school children, would now receive 11 percent of the funding. Representative John Brademas (D.-Ind.), an acknowledged expert on education legislation, argued the case for the Orshansky index in these terms: "Although a few cities do lose some money, a comparison of projected allocations under the new formula with allocations under the present formula . . . shows that most cities can expect to receive significant increases in Title I funds next year."[7] Indeed, the Orshansky formula did increase funding for most of the 100 largest cities.

House Resolution 69, a proposal to "amend and extend" the Elementary and Secondary Education Act, was drafted by the House Education and Labor Committee. The bill incorporated the Orshansky poverty formula for the distribution of Title I funds, and it guaranteed that no school districts would be cut back more than 15 percent from the previous year's allocation. A minority on the committee claimed that the Orshansky index did in fact discriminate against the cities. They claimed that this new formula applied an across-the-board cost-of-living index that understated poverty in high-cost-of-living metropolitan areas. Moreover, the formula was criticized as being too narrowly based in its definition of poverty, excluding such claims on the budgets of poor people as housing, medical care, and income tax. The minority view, using metropolitan county data instead of city data, demonstrated that 35 of the 44 most heavily populated counties in the nation would lose 15 percent of their Title I funds—the maximum loss under the proviso of HR 69 (see Table 7.2).

The heart of the minority case was that the trend in metropolitan development had left the cities with a highly concentrated and less affluent population, and with shrinking economic resources that had fallen behind the cities' burgeoning needs. As a result of the greater need for all kinds of social services, a smaller proportion of the typical city budget was available for education, despite the higher tax rates that exist in metropolitan areas. In effect, the so-called wealthier urban areas, under the Orshansky formula, are the ones that must spend more for services other than education, and consequently must make a greater fiscal effort to obtain the educational services available at less sacrifice in the suburbs (see Table 7.3).

The conclusions of the House urban coalition opposing the Orshansky index involved more than the competing claims on limited resources. They raised the whole issue of equalization of funds as a political strategy of federal intervention:

The consequence of the use of the rural-based Orshansky
index, plus the decrease in A. F. D. C. and the limit on
payment rate is a redistribution of funds away from the
most densely populated jurisdictions. Although the total
number of eligible children increases under this formula
as compared with the present formula, the percent of the
total for population centers decreases as compared with
the present. Since the appropriations level for Title I is
not expected to increase to the level necessary to serve
all of the eligibles, the relative amount that will be made
available to metropolitan areas will decrease. The result
is a dispersion of the funds around the country; . . . the
new formula must be applied to the same sized pie, with

TABLE 7.2

The Impact of the Orshansky Formula on Metropolitan Counties: Dollar Difference between Fiscal Year 1974 Allocation under Current Formula and Fiscal Year 1974 Allocation under New Formula

County	Difference	Percent Loss
California:		
Alameda (Oakland)	-$705,120	-12
Los Angeles	-7,480,150	-15
San Francisco	-646,808	-15
Colorado: Denver	-515,345	-15
Connecticut:		
New Haven	-628,143	-15
Hartford	-631,070	-15
Georgia: Fulton (Atlanta)	-735,572	-15
Illinois: Cook (Chicago)	-7,779,999	-15
Indiana:		
Lake (Gary-East Chicago)	-534,906	-15
St. Joseph (South Bend)	-133,687	-15
Kansas:		
Wyandotte (Kansas City)	-238,806	-15
Sedgewick (Wichita)	-290,686	-15
Kentucky: Jefferson (Louisville)	-754,738	-15
Maryland: Baltimore City	-1,938,183	-15
Massachusetts: Suffolk (Boston)	-1,112,079	-13
Michigan: Wayne (Detroit)	-3,890,005	-15
Minnesota: Hennepin (Minneapolis)	-772,417	-15
Missouri: St. Louis City	-365,833	-6
Nebraska: Douglas (Omaha)	-336,689	13
New Jersey:		
Hudson (Jersey City)	-811,318	-13
Passaic (Paterson)	-624,907	-15
Essex (Newark)	-1,983,153	-15
Mercer (Trenton)	-370,627	-15
New York:		
Erie (Buffalo)	-1,309,828	-15
New York City	-23,156,030	-15
Monroe (Rochester)	-849,801	-15
Onondaga (Syracuse)	-395,771	-14
Westchester (Yonkers)	-930,194	-15
North Carolina:		
Mecklenburg (Charlotte)	-367,220	-15
Forsyth (Winston-Salem)	-274,953	-15
Ohio:		
Summit (Akron)	-334,438	-15
Cuyahoga (Cleveland)	-1,867,259	-15
Franklin (Columbus)	-614,977	-15
Montgomery (Dayton)	-342,917	-15
Oklahoma: Oklahoma (Oklahoma City)	-424,038	-15
Oregon: Multnomah (Portland)	-68,950	-3
Pennsylvania: Philadelphia City	-4,069,704	-15
Rhode Island: Providence	-531,741	-15
South Carolina: Charleston	-423,359	-14
Utah: Salt Lake	-260,352	-13
Virginia:		
Richmond	-367,555	-15
Norfolk	-465,062	-15
Washington	-425,807	-10
Wisconsin: Milwaukee	-952,407	-15

Source: US Congress, House Committee on Education and Labor, 93d Cong. 2d Sess. Congressional Record-House, March 12, 1974, H1711.

smaller slices as the end result. . . . It represents a retreat from the intent of Title I to assist those areas with
large concentrations of need to one more akin to general
assistance to the schools. [8]

The compromise eventually reached in 1974 used a formula for
distribution of Title I funds that included children eligible for aid under
the Orshansky index, plus two-thirds of AFDC recipients above the
poverty line in each district, and poor children not counted in either
category, such as those living in federal institutions. Though the urban
districts were able to cut their losses in the compromise provisions
of the distribution formula, the political parameters of the ESEA had
been set. By 1974, federal aid to secondary and elementary education
amounted to about $4 billion. After 20 years, the federal share of
school costs had doubled, rising from 4 to 8 percent. The bastions of
state and local control over American education had been dented. But
despite the cumulative efforts, the fight for equalizing educational resources moved from Washington to the state and local levels.

TABLE 7.3

Education as a Percentage of Total Expenditures

Urban Area	Percent
Washington, D.C.	26
Outside Washington, D.C.	57
New York City	24
Outside New York City	52
Chicago	33
Outside Chicago	57
Atlanta	39
Outside Atlanta	61
Louisville	40
Outside Louisville	70

Source: US Congress, House Committee on Education and
Labor, 93d Cong. 2d Sess. Congressional Record-House, March
12, 1974, H1711.

THE ROAD FROM THE SERRANO CASE: EQUALIZING SCHOOL FUNDING

Roughly, one in ten school dollars comes from federal aid, five in ten come from local property and other taxes, and four in ten from the states. And it is to the state level that the uphill fight for equalizing school resources has moved in recent years. The variations in school expenditures among subnational units in America are incomprehensible by European standards. Table 7.4 shows per-pupil expenditures among the states. A more microscopic survey of inequities is provided by randomly inspecting some local variations. In 1977, the average state-wide per-pupil expenditure in Connecticut was $1,372. However, the affluent suburb of West Hartford spent $2,059 per pupil, compared with the $858 per-student investment in the poor rural town of Griswold. In Maryland, the per-pupil expenditure in Montgomery County, $1,036, compared favorably with the $635 that Somerset County was able to muster in support of each school child. In New Jersey, property taxes provided as much as $2,300 per student in some districts, and as little as $132 in others. In light of the 1972 U. S. Supreme Court decision, in San Antonio v. Rodriguez, that these methods of funding schools were constitutional, it has remained for the state judicial and legislative structures to cope with the plea for equality that Justice Thurgood Marshall set forth in his dissent in Rodriguez:

> The majority's holding can only be seen as a retreat from our historic commitment to unsupportable acquiescence in a system which deprives children in their earliest years of the chance to reach their full potential as citizens. The Court does this despite the absence of any substantial justification for a scheme which arbitrarily channels educational resources in accordance with the fortuity of the amount of taxable wealth within each district. [9]

The landmark case of Serrano v. Priest (1971) marked a new era of school fiscal reform at the subnational level. Responding to the disparities in taxable school district wealth (see Table 7.5), the California Supreme Court held:

> This funding scheme invidiously discriminates against the poor because it makes the quality of a child's education a function of the wealth of his parents and neighbors. Recognizing that . . . the right of an education in the public school is a fundamental interest which cannot be conditioned on wealth, we can discern no compelling state purpose necessitating the present system of financing. We have concluded

TABLE 7.4

Expenditures per Pupil, by States
(all districts, 1969-70)

	High	Low	Average
Alabama	$ 581	$ 344	$ 463
Alaska	1,810	480	1,330
Arizona	2,223	436	775
Arkansas	664	343	549
California	2,414	569	753
Colorado	2,801	444	735
Connecticut	1,311	499	915
Delaware	1,081	633	891
District of Columbia	—	—	971
Florida	1,036	593	717
Georgia	736	365	589
Hawaii	—	—	984
Idaho	1,763	474	595
Illinois	2,295	391	872
Indiana	965	447	675
Iowa	1,167	592	955
Kansas	1,831	454	731
Kentucky	885	358	580
Louisiana	892	499	749
Maine	1,555	229	723
Maryland	1,037	635	893
Massachusetts	1,281	515	691
Michigan	1,364	491	858
Minnesota	903	370	818
Mississippi	825	283	495
Missouri	1,699	213	720
Montana	1,716	539	802
Nebraska	1,175	623	653
Nevada	1,679	746	753
New Hampshire	1,191	311	687
New Jersey	1,485	400	1,016
New, Mexico	1,183	477	690
New York	1,889	669	1,245
North Carolina	733	467	607

(continued)

Table 7.4 continued

	High	Low	Average
North Dakota	$1,623	$686	$ 665
Ohio	1,685	—	729
Oklahoma	2,566	342	560
Oregon	1,439	399	875
Pennsylvania	1,401	484	892
Rhode Island	1,206	531	885
South Carolina	610	397	615
South Dakota	1,741	350	667
Tennessee	766	315	561
Texas	5,334	264	608
Utah	1,515	533	611
Vermont	1,517	357	1,034
Virginia	1,126	441	753
Washington	3,405	434	873
West Virginia	722	502	646
Wisconsin	1,432	344	941
Wyoming	14,554	618	884

Source: Congressional Quarterly, Education for a Nation (Washington, D.C.: Congressional Quarterly, 1972).

therefore that such a system cannot withstand constitutional challenge and must fall before the equal protection clause.[10]

The policy limitations of the decision, the so-called fiscal neutrality principle, are considerable:

Serrano . . . does not oblige the state to abandon local control of schooling, to provide funds sufficient to compensate for differences in cost of living in different areas, to spend more money, or to help (or hurt) big cities. . . . The constitutional standard that education may not be a function of wealth required only the adoption of a resource distribution formula which assures that poor districts are not short-changed because of their limited taxable resources.

TABLE 7.5

How California's Rich School Districts Raise More Money Through
Less Tax Effort Than Poor School Districts (1968-69)

All Unified School Districts above 1,000 Average Daily Attendance (ADA)	Modified Assured Valuation per ADA (all students)	Current Expenditure per Pupil (ADA)	Tax Rate per $100
Ten Richest Districts			
Average	$34,542	$929.94	$2.82
Range	$28,170-$50,885	$781-$1,232	$2.17-$3.70
Ten Poorest Districts			
Average	$4,144	$609.54	$4.61
Range	$1,883-$4,963	$563-$682	$3.46-$6.10

Source: David L. Kirp, "Inequitable Public School Financing
and the Serrano Case," in Policy and Politics in America, ed. Allan
P. Sindler (Boston: Little, Brown, 1973), p. 89.

> Any formula which distributes education dollars on the
> basis of some rational criteria satisfies Serrano. [11]

The impact of state aid to schools can be seen from the fact that,
in the 20 years between 1950 and 1970, state funds for schools grew
sevenfold. Currently, aggregate state aid to schools constitutes about
40 percent of total funding. The traditional formulas of state aid are
so-called equalizing grants that take into account the fiscal character
of the locality. More than three-fourths of state money provided for
schools are of this type.

The post-Serrano response among judicial and legislative agencies in the states generally moved toward enactment of the fiscal neutrality doctrine—which meant that variations in per-pupil expenditures
could continue in effect, as would efforts to moderately equalize the
distribution of state revenues to the localities. The current situation
stands as follows:

> Alternative models have been produced that are both legal
> and provide adequate equalization; . . . a judicially man-
> ageable standard (equal availability of taxable resources

for each child) and a partial definition of equal educational
opportunity (education may not be a function of wealth other
than the wealth of the state as a whole) have been produced.
The impact of this era is causing school finance scholars
to realize that we can translate the rhetoric governing the
equality of educational opportunity into practice. [12]

The criteria for a funding model that were established by the courts,
and the models recommended by judicial and legislative bodies, are
summarized in Tables 7.6 and 7.7.

Nevertheless, it is naive to expect that major fiscal reform will
occur, given the political and policy agendas of diverse interests in
the states. The issues of district gains and losses, competition with
other social service budgets, and doubts about the social and educational efficacy of the schools pose difficult problems for fiscal reformers:

Educational fiscal reform is the first priority of no one
(except the cottage industry of school finance specialists)
so that the constituency for major change is likely to be
weak. While proposals to decentralize school governance
or levy a state-wide tax for schooling will be resisted by
a host of groups, supporters are fragmented. The so-called
school lobby is typically divided. State education codes effectively separate classroom teachers, counselors, and
school administrators into different camps. Teachers and
parents regularly find themselves battling with each other
over issues of pedagogy and policy. To unite these groups
poses a difficult but not impossible task. [13]

The case of Maryland demonstrates the pitfalls of state fiscal
school reform. [14] In 1971, the Citizens' Commission on Maryland
Government recommended that the state phase in full state funding of
the schools over a period of three years. Three other statewide commissions agreed that the heavy reliance on local property wealth was
the cause of unequal educational opportunity. The situation was compounded by the growth rate of the 1960s and the increased burden on
differential fiscal capacities at the local level. From 1964 to 1969 the
differences between counties spending the least on education and counties spending the most on education had increased to 63 percent. A
combination of political forces, reinforced by concerns about both increased costs of full state assumption of school funding and doubts
about the impact of resource redistribution on the quality of education,
defeated the equalization proposal. Maryland reformers had proposed
a scheme that would base state support on the expenditure level of the

TABLE 7.6

Summation of Criteria for a School Finance Model Established by Courts within One Year of _Serrano_ Decision

| Court Case | Criteria Established by the Courts | | | | | |
	Fiscal Neutrality	Full State Funding	Local Initiative	Local Revenue Must Be Equalized by the State	Variations in Expenditure per Pupil	Flat Grants
Serrano	required	neither prohibited nor required	neither prohibited nor required	required	specifically permitted	neither prohibited nor required
Van Dusartz	required	neither prohibited nor required	neither prohibited nor required	neither prohibited nor required	specifically permitted	neither prohibited nor required
Rodriguez	required	neither prohibited nor required	neither prohibited nor required	required	neither prohibited nor required	neither prohibited nor required
Robinson	required	required	prohibited	not applicable; no local revenue permitted	specifically permitted	prohibited
Sweetwater	required	required	10–15 percent permitted	neither prohibited nor required	specifically permitted	neither prohibited nor required
Hollins	required	neither prohibited nor required	neither prohibited nor required	required	neither prohibited nor required	neither prohibited nor required

Source: Arthur E. Wise and Shelly Weinstein, "The Politics of Inequality," _Phi Delta Kappan_, October 1976, pp. 169–172. Reprinted with permission. Copyright ©1976 by Phi Delta Kappa, Inc.

TABLE 7.7

Recommended Funding Models That Satisfy Court Criteria

Court Criterion and Decisions Endorsing Each Criterion	Recommended Models	
Fiscal neutrality—all decisions	Both California models Delaware model Maryland model	Michigan model New Jersey model New York model
Full state funding—Robinson, Sweetwater	California full-state-assumption model Maryland model	Michigan model New York model
Prohibiting local initiative—Robinson, Sweetwater	California full-state-assumption model Delaware model	Maryland model New York model Michigan model (satisfies Sweetwater only)
Equalization of local revenue by the state—Serrano, Rodriguez, Hollins	California district power equalization model Delaware model	Michigan model New Jersey model
Permitting variations in expenditures per pupil—Serrano, Van Dusartz, Robinson, Sweetwater	Both California models Delaware model Maryland model	Michigan model New Jersey model New York model
Prohibiting flat grants—Robinson	Both California models Delaware model Maryland model	New Jersey model New York model

Source: Arthur E. Wise and Shelly Weinstein, "The Politics of Inequality," Phi Delta Kappan, October 1976, pp. 169–172. Reprinted with permission. Copyright © 1976 by Phi Delta Kappa, Inc.

highest-spending county in the state. Following five years of study, and two years of a conservative plan that retained the old school-aid formula, the consequences for elementary and secondary education in the state were uninspiring:

> Under the plan for full state funding, all education spend-
> ing . . . was to reach $2. 7 billion by 1974-75. In these
> same three years . . . Maryland's education spending . . .
> exceeded $3. 1 billion. The full-funding plan capped per
> pupil costs at $1,104 by 1974. The actual state average
> per pupil expenditure increased by almost 50% and the
> state's share of these rising costs had increased by 2%.
> . . . In 1969 the wealthiest county was three times richer
> than the poorest; in 1975 it was four times richer. In 1969
> the highest spending county expended 63% more per pupil
> than did the lowest spending county. In 1975, the highest
> spending county expended 95% more per pupil than the low-
> est spending county. [15]

The technical attributes of various equalization formulas are beyond the purview of this policy discussion; it is sufficient to point out the impact on low-income and big-city districts under varying degrees of state reform.

The Maryland case is illustrative of a low-scale reform program. Baltimore City's $6. 09 property tax rate is the highest in the state. Suburban Montgomery County ranks fourteenth in the state with a $2. 53 property tax rate. In 1975 Montgomery County had $575 per pupil available while Baltimore City, Maryland's fourth poorest school district, spent $1,196 per pupil.

Modest reform was carried out in the state of California, which employs a guaranteed minimum per school district at a specified tax level. In 1972 the California legislature increased the state's base support level per student, limited additional school spending by wealthy districts, and authorized additional compensatory education funds. The average increase in state aid was 37 percent in 1974; however, large cities gained less in school aid. Aid to Los Angeles and San Diego increased approximately 20 percent, while Long Beach and San Francisco gained nothing from the additional state aid. [16]

An expansive reform program was pursued in Kansas, where legislation considered both district wealth and tax effort in school funding. Consequently, cities received an average increase of 129 percent in state aid during 1974, compared with a statewide increase of 81 percent. Moreover, local school property taxes in cities decreased 24 percent, compared with a 6 percent statewide decline. A comparable Wisconsin enactment significantly aided Milwaukee, Racine, and Green Bay, placing them above the state average in school aid.

The development of equalization formulas cannot be gauged without consideration of individual state politics. In general, we doubt that any mechanical Robin Hood formula for redistributing school aid from rich to poor districts has much chance of uniform support. The more likely case is a series of incremental changes, applying different mixes of fiscal and policy concepts from the litanies of school finance.

The Reform Program

Between 1970 and 1975, 20 states revised their programs of state aid to school districts. Many more are reevaluating existing programs. States have a variety of alternatives from which to choose, ranging from full state assumption of funding, to schemes that aim simply to reduce disparities in resources among existing school districts, to schemes that redraw school district boundaries in order to equalize the potential tax base. Most states have opted for less dramatic, middle-of-the-road options whereby they develop new methods of equalizing resources without changing local boundaries or limiting local autonomy.

The most popular scheme has been the power-equalizing approach. This does not seek to guarantee that all school districts in the state spend the same amount on each of their respective pupils. Rather, it guarantees that the amount of revenue raised by any particular tax rate in one school district will be equal to that raised in another school district, regardless of the potential tax base of the districts. That is, equal tax rates are designed to produce equal per-pupil expenditure, with the state subsidizing the poorer districts up to the spending level of the richer. Pupils are not penalized simply by living in a poorer district. Rather, the resources available for their education are determined locally by the decision of the school boards and voters about the appropriate rate of taxation that should be levied in the community. Fiscal neutrality is thus achieved; yet local autonomy is protected with discretion still left to the school district to vary its revenue policies.

However, while such reform schemes have improved the financial situation of many school districts and their taxpayers, they fall far short of achieving equality of provision for the individual pupil, especially in urban areas. District power equalization does not adequately handle the problems of the limited fiscal capacity of central cities. In particular, it does not take into account the problem of municipal overburden, whereby central city residents face higher tax burdens to support a broader range of municipal services than do suburbanites. As a result, cities must tax at a lower level for education purposes in order to leave capacity for other services. Power equalization schemes guarantee that any particular rate of taxation in the central city produces the same amount of revenue as it would in the suburbs, regardless of property values. But they are of limited equalizing effect when city districts have limited capacity to raise tax rates while suburban districts can easily levy the necessary higher taxation rates to produce more revenues for spending on individual pupils. Only five state finance programs make any allowance for these extraordinary noneducational burdens facing central cities.

Also, power equalization schemes retain an element of regressivity because they are based on property values rather than on family income. Identical tax rates on identically assessed property will absorb a larger proportion of the resources of the lower-income family in the central cities than those of the higher-income family in the suburbs. Only five states employ income as a measure of community wealth. All others depend upon property wealth.

Power equalization schemes also make no allowance for cost differentials, in terms of salaries, land costs, insurance, and maintenance costs, or for the greater educational needs of socially disadvantaged central city school children, which make it more expensive for cities to provide the same level of services available in suburban districts. Only one state, Florida, has included an allowance for such cost differentials in its funding program. Programs in 19 states do offer categorical aid as compensatory educational funding, but overall major inequities remain in the allocation of resources among urban and suburban areas. The judgment of the National Conference of State Legislators was that although "not unkind to urban school districts," when it came to "defining fiscal need in terms other than simply poor, and attempting to meet those more comprehensively defined needs, the record of the states is not so good."[17] On balance, their reform programs have not had a major impact upon the position of financially stretched central city school systems and their pupils.

THE FUTURE

Future efforts to achieve school finance reform will probably focus upon a broader range of issues. Initially, reformers concentrated on a narrower range of issues that covered the inequities of the property tax and the fiscal neutrality doctrines, because they were susceptible to judicial remedy, which seemed the most profitable short-term strategy. However, even if such reforms are introduced, many problems will remain, as we have seen. In the final analysis, reform must focus upon the range and quality of educational services children receive and upon the impact of state policies on them, rather than upon the narrower taxation and revenue dimensions of state programs. But to approach equality, more attention will need to be paid to the general structure of revenue and taxation at local government levels.

There are, however, a number of major barriers that stand in the path of reform, creating pessimism about the fate of school finance reform. [18] For example, most reforms have occurred between 1970 and 1973. Few have occurred since that time. Also a number of states that did introduce reform programs in the early 1970s are having great difficulty in funding them five years later. And in 1977, in Maine, voters in a referendum actually rejected the reform program that the state had introduced several years earlier on the ground that it had inhibited local autonomy. The primary barriers to further reform remained financial ones, however, since reform of any kind will inevitably involve higher expenditure levels. Existing commitments to school districts would prevent the adoption of any scheme that simply redistributed existing levels of resources. And in any case, equalizing district expenditures implies levying higher taxes to bring the expenditure of the poorer districts up to that of the richer ones.

And objections to increased local expenditure are already being raised. In part, it is simply the growing reluctance of taxpayers to pay more, particularly as assessing authorities in many metropolitan areas are beginning to increase the tax assessment on residential property to keep taxes in line with increases in market value in an inflationary era. The passage of Proposition 13, severely limiting levels of property taxes in California, is the most dramatic and important case of taxpayer backlash, with enormous implications for school districts. More generally, the impact of the economic recession, rising inflation, and the cost of government services will severely restrain the amount of new state money available for funding equalization programs. Indeed, given that many states were able to introduce reform programs only because they enjoyed a temporary revenue surplus in the early 1970s, the financial barriers to reform loom large.

And even if fiscal problems were eliminated, political barriers to reform would remain. Increased state involvement in school financing creates fears that state control will follow in other areas of education, directly conflicting with the still-intense commitment to local control found at the local level, and makes state action less likely.

In the late 1970s the reform of school finances remains an important issue in educational politics. But it seems unlikely that there will be any major state initiatives to reduce the problem of the poverty of educational opportunity for children in the poorer school districts. As in other areas of education, the focus of attention is more likely to shift away from problems of raising new revenues to secure greater equality, and toward those of distributing existing revenues. In this context, the most successful political coalition is likely to be, not that of potential beneficiaries of reform—that is, central city or rural school districts—but rather, that of the comfortable suburbs combined with business interests. In this case, as Joel Berke has pointed out, the most likely result will not be reform, but "a reduction in property tax burdens for many communities, accompanied by a lack of attention to noneducational tax pressures and to differences in educational need."[19] In this context, power equalization schemes, if less than wholly adequate, may seem an increasingly attractive option.

The Impact of Educational Reform

The controversy about the educational and social impact of reform is firmly implanted in American politics. The thesis that schools neither educate nor perform any other progressive social function is increasingly disseminated among the American public.[20] We cannot say, for instance, that Baltimore City's place at the bottom of all Maryland school districts in language- and mathematics-test scores was caused by its current decline to the twenty-first position among 24 districts in per-pupil spending. Nor, to return to our discussion of federal education policy, can we show that Baltimore City's educational system would improve to the level of Montgomery County's system were Montgomery County's 120,000 students denied their $6.2 million in federal aid, and Baltimore City's 173,000 students reinforced with these monies to augment their $7 million in federal aid.

What can be said is that American central cities—and poor rural areas as well—bear the brunt of unemployment, social pathology, and stunted life chances. Continued debate about the size of the federal and state assumption of educational costs inevitably comes down to hard allocative decisions in the dispersing of finite resources. The concept of equality of opportunity has become a charade in a nation where the well off can purchase the amenities of schooling simply because they reside in prosperous suburbs. Since increased resources do not necessarily improve the quality of education, children of modest or inadequate means should also have the opportunity to participate in enriching experiences.

Furthermore, frustration will only increase by insisting upon the equally illusionary doctrine that only equality of educational outcomes really matters. Volumes have been written in efforts to define equality of outcome. More critical is the reality of the pattern of individual preferences and mobility, whereby the choice of residence and school district provides evidence of success in the American way of life. Proposals for power equalizing more readily mix the ideal with the politically obtainable. Power-equalizing schemes mean that rich and poor districts that taxed themselves at the same rate would have equal amounts to spend per pupil.[21] The Wisconsin scheme, in which power equalizing is combined with compensatory state aid to disadvantaged students highly concentrated in the cities, is an exemplary model.

The various equalization proposals are most likely to bear fruit within the context of consolidated educational agencies and programs at the state and federal levels. The diversity of categorical education programs at the state and federal levels enhances the ability of particular districts to acquire additional dollars. Indeed, too often, wealthier districts have the administrative skills that provide them with an edge in the competition for funds from a myriad of state and federal sources. For example, Maryland's wealthiest county, Montgomery, receives the largest per-pupil share of federal-impact and Head Start funds. It is for this reason that a federal Department of Education ought to be established, because it is a likely environment in which to consolidate educational programs rooted in equalization and need formulas. For, in the long run, decentralized state and federal educational measures neglect the centers of educational need.

The objective is to set national and state standards of educational need that are tied to dollar allocations. Once this is accomplished, the surplus wealth of the suburbs will not directly deny adequate educational services for their less well-off neighbors. Communities will be free to decide how much added tax effort will be made at the local level. Moreover, the stratified consequences of heavy reliance on local property taxes will be ameliorated by new government standards for the provision of educational need and dollars to sustain the schools. A frontal assault on "local control" has proven to be a failure. [22] It is possible to cap the decade of educational reform at the federal and subnational levels with a stronger base of service and fiscal resources that more nearly realizes the historic commitment of equal educational opportunity and compensates for the circumstances of family income and domicile.

Public Law 93-380 is a step in this direction, as it provides federal aid to the states for the administration and development of equalization plans. A categoric aid program to slow the growth of interstate differentials in school expenditures is under construction. Between 1970 and 1975 the difference in per-pupil expenditure between the most generous state and the least generous state increased from $837 to $1,112, in constant dollars.

Taking a broad historical overview, the problems of educational opportunity in America must be set alongside the considerable accomplishments in this area. Only Sweden exceeds the United States in per-capita expenditures on elementary and secondary education among the highly developed industrial democracies. The fact that America spends about $62 billion on its schools at the elementary level (only 6.5 percent of our GNP) means there is much room for improvement. At the elementary level, the performance of American school children generally ranks favorably with those in other parts of the postindustrial world. And if American performance at the secondary level lags in such areas as science, it must be noted that 75 percent of American high school students completed a recent international educational evaluation test, compared with much smaller proportions of the comparable population elsewhere—29 percent in France, 9 percent in Germany, for example. Moreover, the constant dollar expenditure has risen consistently in the United States since 1968.[23] It is in this context of the enormous scale and expectation regarding education that the inequities of the case must be considered and dealt with. Indeed, out commitment to universal education partially accounts for differential expenditures, in that, between 1970 and 1975, while national expenditures rose, those in southeastern states remained stationary, in constant dollars. Consequently, the efforts to secure a greater educational share of tax dollars at all levels must be linked to fail-safe policies that maintain adequate base support levels in the least affluent states and school districts.

NOTES

1. Robert Bendiner, Obstacle Course on Capitol Hill (New York: McGraw-Hill, 1964).
2. US Congress, House, Committee on Education and Labor, Aid to Elementary and Secondary Education, Hearings Before the General Subcommittee on Education, Committee on Education and Labor, House of Representatives, 89th Cong., 1st sess. (Washington, D.C.: US Government Printing Office, 1965).
3. Michael S. March, Federal Programs for Human Resource Development: A Compendium of Papers, Joint Economic Committee, 90th Cong. 2d sess., 1968.
4. US, Congress, House, Committee on Education and Labor, Consideration of H.R. 93-803 To Amend the 1965 E.S.E.A., February 21, 1974.
5. Joel Spring, The Sorting Machine: National Educational Policy Since 1945 (New York: David McKay, 1976).
6. Quoted in Congressional Quarterly, April 24, 1976, p. 968.
7. US, Congress, House, Congressional Record, March 6, 1974, H1530.
8. US, Congress, House, Congressional Record, March 12, 1974, H1711.
9. San Antonio v. Rodriguez, 411 U.S., 1973.
10. Quoted in Congressional Quarterly, Education for a Nation (Washington, D.C.: Congressional Quarterly, 1972), p. 4.
11. David L. Kirp, "Inequitable Public School Financing and the Serrano Case," in Policy and Politics in America, ed. Allan P. Sindler (Boston: Little, Brown, 1973), p. 89.

12. Robert J. Wynkoop, "Prognosis for Change in State Finance Plans," Education Administration Quarterly 10, no. 3 (Autumn, 1974): 20-32.

13. Kirp, op. cit. , p. 109.

14. This discussion is based on Arthur E. Wise and Shelly Weinstein, "The Politics of Inequality," Phi Delta Kappan, October 1976, pp. 169-72.

15. Ibid. , p. 17.

16. The examples of modest and low-scale reform programs are from Austin D. Swanson and Richard A. King, "The Impact of the Courts on the Financing of Public Schools in Large Cities," Urban Education 11, no. 2, (July 1976): 151-65.

17. John J. Callaman and William H. Wilken, eds. , School Finance Reform: a Legislator's Handbook (Washington, D. C. : National Conference of State Legislatures, 1976), p. 46.

18. See Donna E. Shaala and Mary Frase Williams, "Political Perspectives on Recent Efforts to Reform School Finance," in Political Science and School Politics, ed. Frederick M. Wirt and Samuel K. Gove (Lexington, Mass. : D. C. Heath, 1976), pp. 69-82.

19. Joel S. Berke, Answers to Inequity (Berkeley: McCutchan, 1974), p. 119.

20. See Diane Ravitch, "The Revisionists Revisited: Studies in the Historiography of American Education," Proceedings of the National Academy of Education 4 (1977) for an insightful critique of the view that schools are instruments of a capitalist society.

21. The seminal work is John E. Coons, William H. Clune, and Stephen Sugarman, Private Wealth and Public Education (Cambridge: Harvard University Press, 1973).

22. See Jerome T. Murphy, "The Education Bureaucracies Implement Novel Policy: The Politics of Title I of E. S. E. A. ," in Sindler, op. cit. , pp. 161-98; David Rodgers, 110 Livingston Street (New York: Random House, 1968).

23. Statistics in this concluding section are from the National Center for Educational Statistics, The Condition of Education (Washington, D. C. : US Government Printing Office, 1976).

8

CONCLUSION:
COMMON POLICY THEMES

This study has examined some recent developments in educational policy and politics in Britain and America. It has suggested that shared underlying policy themes can be found. We have argued that, despite the obvious institutional and cultural diversity, comparable climates of opinion have emerged in both countries during the 1970s as decision makers, in an era of financial austerity and retrenchment, have struggled with the implications of the programs of the 1960s, with their commitment to expanded educational provision and expanded equality of opportunity. The dilemmas involved in sustaining a rapidly expanded pattern of opportunities with limited funds has produced, in both countries, comparable tendencies and policy responses, which we have called policy centralization and policy leveling.

It is clear that in the 1970s, the unqualified role of education as a growth vehicle in advanced industrial societies no longer exists. Education's societal mission is clouded, responsive to competitive and often contradictory demands, and faces increasing external competition from other items on national social budgets. Political elites have lost confidence in the ability of education to meet the social and economic demands placed upon it. Although neither the anticipated increases in economic efficiency nor social justice has resulted from the reform efforts of the 1960s, the public expectations that were encouraged by official policies during that earlier period have not declined. And decision makers are now faced with the problems of coping with sustained demand for education with reduced public resources.

POLICY CENTRALIZATION

One response to this new situation has been a growth in the power of central government and in bureaucratic control, with decision makers struggling to match priorities with limited resources.

In both countries a consensus has emerged that decision makers at the subnational or local level cannot respond adequately to centrally determined national goals and, in particular, cannot be relied upon to exercise rigorous control over costs and expenditure. To achieve this control, decision-making power has been progressively shifted upward in the governmental and administrative hierarchy. Thus in Britain, in higher education the mass colleges of the public sector have been favored not only because their costs are assumed to be lower, but because central control over them could be exercised more directly than was the case among the meritocratic universities, where a diffuse model of power, exemplified by the UGC, prevailed. But in time, as we have seen, even that model has succumbed to the imperatives of a determined central bureaucracy.

In the United States, similar motives inspired the expansion of student aid, as opposed to institutional aid programs. Even though the federal government cannot directly control the individual consumer, student aid still seemed, to central decision makers, a more economical method of controlling system growth than the apparently more direct institutional aid model. This model, encouraged by federal requirements for the introduction of planning commissions, has become an exemplar for state policies also. At the state level, again, we have charted an upward shift in power in the administrative hierarchy; individual faculty and departments have lost authority to higher-level bodies in the name of rationalized decision making.

At the school level, too, we have found growing central power, although designed as much to increase equality of opportunity as to control expenditure. However, it would be naive to argue that the consequences of centralization have been identical in the two countries. In Britain, the shift in policy has produced a much more powerful DES which increasingly intervenes in the internal life of schools as well as in the broader issues of institutional framework. In the United States, increased federal funding, as well as federal efforts to enforce school desegregation, mark a similar drift toward the nationalization of educational politics. But the forces of pluralism, decentralization, and commitment to the local autonomy endemic to the federal system have more successfully resisted the emergence of an all-powerful central Office of Education and the imposition of central power. At present, localities are still able to resist federal initiatives in many ways. As Jerome Murphy has written in regard to the problems of more general educational reform in the United States, "the federal system—with its dispersion of power and control—not only permits but encourages the evasion and dilution of federal reform, making it nearly impossible for the federal administrator to impose program priorities; those not diluted by congressional intervention can be ignored during state and local implementation."[1] Nevertheless, the long-term drift is toward, rather than away from, national standards. The continuing consolidation of school districts, the growing dominance of textbook publishers over the curriculum, the impact of court decisions on a variety of critical issues, the emergence of national education lobby groups combined with federal initiatives—all of this suggests that policy differences between localities are diminishing, rather than increasing, over time. The proposal to create a separate cabinet status for the Office of Education, if implemented, would surely exaggerate recent trends. And whatever variation remains, it is clear that a more centralized bureaucratic power system has developed in both Washington and London, and that increasingly, the DES and a cluster of federal agencies will determine the content of education policy and the allocation of scarce resources.

POLICY LEVELING

This growth in central decision making has aided a second trend that we have identified as policy leveling, which results from the effort to accommodate continued demands for equal educational opportunity with diminishing economic resources. This has become particularly evident at the postsecondary level. Throughout the affluent 1960s, support for expanded educational opportunities could be integrated with continued support for selective elite institutions. But in the 1970s, in a period of financial austerity, it has become increasingly difficult to sustain both these goals. In this situation, powerful central decision makers have opted for the strategy of policy leveling, in which political and financial support for cheaper mass institutions is increased at the cost of the more expensive, prestigious elite institutions. The effort to achieve equality of opportunity in the face of reduced resources has thus created a new array of problems and conflicts within the educational world. Advocates of affirmative action and comprehensive education, for example, are faced with renewed opposition. There are increased internal conflicts as institutions compete for resources with the new institutions that have been fostered by, and are dependent upon, the national education bureaucracies—the polytechnics, the community colleges, and vocational institutions.

Most significantly, the unanticipated consequences of public policies continue to shape the distribution of power, money, and educational opportunities. Nobody expected that British universities would suffer in order to fulfill the binary scheme. Nobody expected that quality universities and middle-class academic achievers would pay the costs of American Basic Educational Opportunity Grants and affirmative action. Yet these are the consequences of new social pressures and economic misfortunes. In retrospect, both the binary policy and the US higher education policy had hidden price tags—costs that became manifest years after the original mandates. Both in Britain and the United States, governments have failed to develop a long-term strategy for the support of higher education that protects the interests of both mass and elite institutions. Rather, policy has reacted to short-term criteria, like changing market demand or rising costs, which do not necessarily form a suitable basis for long-term planning. Yet demand for higher education fluctuates in response not only to consumer needs but also to public policies. Retrenchment in public policies itself causes changes in future demands regarding both the nature and extent of educational opportunities. A coherent national policy statement would take such factors into account, but would also pay greater attention to other goals of education—in particular, the preservation of institutions that have long-term ambitions and significance. Universities committed to scholarship and research that have critical implications for both the social and economic well-being of the country have equally valid claims on the public purse, and at least should not have their fate determined solely by the vicissitudes of the marketplace. Even in the private American sector, government subsidies are of enormous significance, and policy should be more attuned to the consequences of the changing patterns of support.

At the school level, we have also witnessed a search for equality of opportunity. That in itself may be regarded as a desirable social goal. But again, a greater awareness of the unintended impact of such public policies might be required. One does not need a defense of elite schools to observe that public policies should be sensitive to their needs, to avoid penalizing intellectually able children of all social classes, for the sake of the formal state of equality. Indeed, evidence suggests that it is extremely difficult for governments to develop policies guaranteeing equal opportunity for underprivileged groups. That in itself should not prevent the search for more policies. But as we have suggested, governments should be aware of the unintended process of resegregation in the educational sector that the search for equality may produce.

The policy innovations of the late 1960s, Labour's bid for social justice, and the Great Society initiatives required at least a decade to play themselves out. However, it is striking how little conservative rule in both the United Kingdom and United States has altered the major drift of national education policies. In the end, the national bureaucracies exerted consistent influence in implementing, for example, the binary scheme and in expanding student aid as a major source of US federal aid. The future remains uncertain, but the evidence suggests that this dialectical stress between the productive and social justice goals of education policy will continue to plague policy makers in both countries. The social ideology of bureaucracies will continue to influence the distribution of life chances, the subsidies, individual cases, and inducements that shape the educational future in Britain and America.

NOTE

1. Jerome T. Murphy, "Title I of E. S. E. A. : The Politics of Implementing Federal Education Reform," Harvard Educational Review 41, no. 1 (1971), p. 60.

EPILOGUE

This study in Anglo-American education policy relates to the burgeoning field of comparative policy studies. We hope that our concern with bicultural education policy has broader application, for interests in education in other countries and for other public policy areas. First, comparative policy studies must build upon rich mines of social science knowledge. In our case, political theory, public administration, and education policy provided the mineral deposit for our intellectual excursion. Second, the issue of what to compare is one that is eventually decided by the core concerns of the scholar. The authors began with the observations that, despite the vast structural differences between British and American polities, there were quite similar concerns among educational policy makers and institutions in both countries. We used the term "policy agenda" to connote these convergencies, and proceeded to identify three themes that connected them to our broader interests.

In summary form, we found that despite equalization measures, the social expectations of education and the availability of resources created a situation of increasing dialectical tension. Consequently, there was policy strain resulting from the demands for, and supply of, educational opportunities, and their anticipated social benefits. Policy bureaucrats responded to this dilemma by resorting to policy leveling (or "policy containment," in Martin Rein's term). This meant that a variation of Gresham's law was applied in the allocation of public resources to education, by which cheaper goods tended to drive out dearer goods. The irony is that, in the name of enhanced educational and social equality, those educational processes and institutions most likely to increase social mobility for the disadvantaged were progressively devalued. Moreover, the critical by-product of this policy icy drama is the increased centralization of national education policy (at different stages of development in the two countries) and the expansion of hegemony among the bureaucracies in London and Washington. Concomitantly, there is a progressive diminution of the power of various pluralistic institutions, ranging from the University Grants Committee in Britain to higher education interest groups in the United States, and there are more concentrated uses of governmental power. Whether it be student-aid policy or affirmative action, the long-term consequence is the decline of subnational autonomy, from the campus to the local authority.

The broader point is that, regardless of particular concerns, comparative education policy must strive to enlighten us about the fundamental political and intellectual issues of the day. For example, consider the enduring fit between educational and occupational outcomes. Despite recent reforms, West German education remains a hierarchical arrangement in which university admission follows a highly selective gymnasium education and the successful completion of the Abitur examination (itself based on gymnasium studies). To equalitarian American eyes, this system appears to be terribly unfair. However, the West Germans have matched educational attainment with slots in their political economy. Graduates of technical high schools and colleges are trained for good jobs, without invidious comparisons being made with university graduates bound for the professions and the civil service. No such system exists in America, because of strong political forces that would oppose it. Consequently, the American differential-opportunity system works only when larger shares of the GNP are pumped into education.

It has great difficulty coping with downward spirals or retrenchment policies. The pressure for more equalitarian outcomes—fashionable at the moment—impairs the system's ability to match educational outcomes with available occupational opportunities. Thus, our educational institutions—ranging from high schools to community colleges and beyond—are torn between providing usable job skills and helping fulfill the quest for individual upward mobility, sought by many and achieved by few. In the end, there are a limited number of command posts or good jobs in each country. The core policy difference is in the social arrangements that differentiate the two systems.

Or consider the clash between meritocratic and equalitarian norms in the rewarding of educational and social ambitions. Our evidence convinces us that there is a systematic bias against meritocratic institutions and processes within the policy-leveling central bureaucracies, be they the British Department of Education and Science or the US Civil Rights Division. In the end, it is impossible to practice policy leveling and fulfill vast equalitarian expectations. Some of this is beyond the realm of the educational system, namely, the progress or recession that is operative in the national political economy. But beyond that, the weakening of meritocratic institutions (American state universities, British redbricks) has two inequalitarian consequences. It cheapens the value of a degree from heretofore prestigious institutions that have provided much social mobility for the working class and racial minorities; and it reinforces the social distance between elite educational bastions (private schools and colleges, Oxbridge, the Ivy League) and the rest of the educational sector. Since elite admissions and credentialing are still highly influenced by acquired wealth and power (although less so than in previous generations), it follows that the range of social opportunity has been reduced. And historically, it is in social and educational advances among the broad middle class that the way has been paved for gains by the culturally and educationally deprived. Moreover, the added price that must be paid in the search for more equality is the enhancement of centralized political power. It is a game that the wealthy can ignore and the upper middle class (those who man the public bureaucracies and send their children to Sussex or Princeton) can profit from, but it is a zero-sum game for the great mass of the citizenry.

Moreover, American students can apply much of what is learned in cross-cultural policy studies, including new insights into their own polity. Consider the Bakke decision and the whole area of affirmative action. The West Germans, despite great pressure on their university-admission capacities, reserve 15 percent of the places for "social hardship" cases; this is usually a polite way of saying "working-class" students—a connotation less amenable to American social discourse. If the University of California-Davis had applied its special social-hardship program in the same way, there would have been no Supreme Court decision in the Bakke case. That is to say, admitting some poor white students would have not only avoided the controversy, but would have enabled racial minorities to gain most (but not all) of the admission advantages built into the special-admissions program.

Or consider the relationship made between educational investment and human capital—an argument or justification for educational expansion that was popular a decade ago. The Swedish case is illuminating here, because it bears much resemblance to the American concern with social equality. The Swedes progressively reformed their secondary and higher education systems through open admissions, study grants, mobility, with pay, between the job and the classroom, and open faculties geared to broad interests (comparable to the land-grant college experience with extension and continuing education programs). When Swedish productivity fell in the 1970s, the government had no choice but to adjust its manpower planning to the new realities. The professional programs (medicine, etc.) received larger shares of available resources at the expense of the open faculties (liberal arts, humanities). The net result was to increase the educational differences between the middle and working classes, since the latter are much scarcer in professional education than in the open subjects. The situation is relevant to the United States in that, in our differential-opportunity system, career education programs are doomed to failure so long as they do not follow economic principles about supply and demand. This is a point that has never been lost among the professional guilds that control admission to our law, medical, and other highly prestigious (and profitable) institutions. Unlike the expansive 1960s, the present retrenchment means that application of manpower for a postindustrial society reduces goals of social equality in the name of technological and productive priorities. It is this realization that, in part, animated the British expansion of their polytechnics, which we have described in this book. The trouble was that the most technically efficient institutions (the colleges of advanced technology) had already been given university status before the implementation of the binary scheme. Consequently, government policy makers are left the seemingly impossible task of increasing economic development, with the most underdeveloped institutions and social groups left under their purview. The fatal flaw, in attempts to reconcile social equality with retrenchment-era human-capital theory, is to ignore the fact that corporate capitalism advances its production in the most sophisticated and technical areas—and is therefore interested in the Massachusetts Institute of Technology and the California Institute of Technology, not in liberal arts or community college education. Of course, one may reject this materialistic view of human education, with appropriate quotes from Spinoza and Faulkner. The cold truth is that once policy rationalization is dominant, and centralized in government hands, laws of economics have more influence on bureaucratic imperatives than liberal arts sentiments.

There is, in all this, a necessity to disconnect the synthesis between educational equality and economic advancement. Both in Britain, with Fabian variations, and in the US differential-opportunity system, it is now the case that one must pay the price of reduced economic gain in order to enhance social equality, or the reverse is true. The entire case of Britain supports the proposition; and almost every American head of a complex state higher education system has experienced it. Put differently, the economic payoff is usually in the hard sciences and engineering programs that intersect with major economic forces of a state. The social pressure comes from the racial minorities and other forces in the liberal arts college. It is at least worth speculating about the possibility that, social equality advocates in government bureaus, in an effort to increase the liberal arts college's share of advanced capitalism, actually impede its progress, and consequently reduce the shares in which their constituents are expected to profit.

Finally, there is the broad issue of structural (and governmental) organization and the implementation of educational policy. We need to look more closely at the ways these arrangements are made and broken, and at the long-term consequence for the educational sphere. Consider some of the variations of this structural-outcome inquiry. Both America and West Germany have federal systems. Nevertheless, there exists in West Germany something that can be called the Bonn confederation—that is to say, an interlocking, overlapping network of Bund (federal) and Lander (state, ministries, and other actors. No such arrangement exists in the United States, with our federal system. Nor is the difference explained in terms of political disagreements inhibiting policy coordination. In fact, the Germans avoid political disagreements about the degree of growth in comprehensive education (equality), the precise number of secondary students that should go on to universities, and other structural matters. They then fashion a compromise based on a common interest—for example, a better teacher-pupil ratio in the liberal, Protestant, Social Democratic north as well as in the conservative, Catholic, Christian Democratic south; something that representatives from Hesse and Bavaria can mutually agree to. The main difference, as compared with the American case, lies not in federalism, political parties, or other such categories, but in the greater control of the educational system available to higher civil servants (administrators) in Bonn as compared with Washington. This illustrative case suggests one of the enduring reasons for the frustration of coordinated policy in American education (we are still trying to fashion a Department of Education). That reason is the enormous—almost insurmountable—difficulty of aggregating enough power, money, and prestige anywhere within our educational system, at any governmental level. Coming at the proposition from the other side, the difficulty is often the result of American antibureaucratic, antigovernmental, antiprofessional power aggrandizement that is self-frustrating. The end result of much American policy making is more government, more bureaucracy (one agency watches the other), more professionals on the HEW payroll. The West Germans have centralized agreement, worked around structural and policy differences. We end up with fragmented centralization with chunks of power spread among considerably influential agencies and their congressional and constituency allies. From this vantage point, the American system is less pluralistic than centrally fragmented, as more power and budgetary control passes up the line from the campus to the state higher education board, or from local units to Washington. From the vantage point of a school superintendent or a university president, the ominous flow of policy directives from multiple state and federal agencies certainly matches the more centralized power of the Department of Education and Science that confronts the Sheffield local educational authority or Bristol University.

The promise of future comparative educational policy studies lies in explorations such as these, which flesh out the intricate connections among institutional, policy, and distribution arrangements. The world of the school principal or college administrator differs from that of the secretary of education in London or the Secretary of HEW in Washington. Nevertheless, we strongly suggest the need to connect concerns about policies and institutional or ideological arrangements with a contextual setting in which their cumulative, and often diverse, impact can be sorted out. The extent to which this study contributes to those efforts is reward enough for our efforts to better understand the transatlantic connection between Whitehall and Washington, and between the comprehensive-school movement and the vast unsettling of established practices in the name of racial and status aspirations in America.

BIBLIOGRAPHY

BRITISH EDUCATION POLICY

Benn, Caroline, and Brian Simon. Half Way There: A Report on the Comprehensives. London: McGraw-Hill, 1972.

Burgess, Tyrrell. A Guide to English Schools. Penguin Books, 1972.

Burgess, Tyrrell, and John Pratt. The Colleges of Advanced Technology. London: Penguin Press, 1974.

Cockburn, Alexander, and Robin Blackburn, eds. Student Power. London: Penguin Press, 1969.

Central Advisory Committee for Education. Children and Their Primary Schools. 2 vols. London: Her Majesty's Stationery Office, 1969.

Committee on Higher Education. Higher Education: Report. London: Her Majesty's Stationery Office, 1968.

Council for Education. Department of Education and Science. Half Our Future. London: Her Majesty's Stationery Office, 1963.

Dale, R. R., and S. Griffith. Down Stream: Failure in the Grammar School. London: Routledge and Kegan Paul, 1965.

Fowler, Gerlad, and Vera Morris. Decision Making in British Education. London: Heinemann, 1973.

Glennester, Howard. Social Service Budgets and Social Policy. London: Allen and Unwin, 1975.

Halsey, A. H., and Martin Trow. The British Academics. London: Faber and Faber, 1971.

Heclo, Hugh. Modern Social Politics in Britain and Sweden. Yale University Press, 1974.

Heclo, Hugh, and Aaron Wildavsky. The Private Government of Public Money. London: Macmillan, 1974.

Jackson, Brian. Streaming: An Education in Miniature. London: Routledge and Kegan Paul, 1965.

Karabel, Jerome, and A. H. Halsey, eds. Power and Ideology in Education. New York: Oxford University Press, 1977.

Kavanagh, Dennis, and Richard Rose. New Trends in British Politics. Beverly Hills: Sage Publications, 1977.

Kogan, Maurice. The Government of Education. New York: Citation Press, 1971.

____. Education Policy Making. London: Allen and Unwin, 1975.

Manzer, R. A. Teachers and Politics. Manchester: Manchester University Press, 1970.

Holly, Douglas, ed. Education or Dominance? Newton Upper Falls, Mass.: Arrow Press, 1974.

Organization for Economic Cooperation and Development. Educational Development Strategy in England and Wales. Paris: OECD, 1975.

Parkinson, Michael. The Labour Party and the Organization of Secondary Education. London: Routledge, Kegan Paul, 1970.

Partridge, John. Life in a Secondary Modern School. London: Pelican Press, 1970.

Pratt, John, and Tyrrell Burgess. The Polytechnics. London: Pitman, 1974.

Rose, Richard. Politics in England. Boston: Little, Brown, 1974.

Sampson, Anthony. The New Anatomy of Britain. New York: Stein and Day, 1972.

Spolton, Lewis. The Upper Secondary School. London: Pergamon Press, 1967.

Willis, Paul. Learning to Labour. London: Saxon House, 1977.

AMERICAN EDUCATION POLICY

Agger, Robert, et al. Who Will Rule the Schools? Belmont, Calif.: Wadsworth, 1971.

Averich, Harvey. How Effective Is Schooling? Santa Monica: Rand Corp., 1971.

Berg, Ivor. The Great Training Robbery. Boston: Beacon Press, 1971.

Berke, Joel. Answers to Inequity. Berkeley: McCutchan, 1974.

Brenneman, David, and Chester Finn. Public Policy and Private Higher Education. Washington, D.C.: Brookings Institution, 1978.

Carnegie Council on Policy Studies in Education. The Federal Role in Post-Secondary Education. San Francisco: Jossey-Bass, 1975.

Carnegie Foundation for the Advancement of Teaching. More Than Survival: Prospects for Higher Education in a Period of Uncertainty. San Francisco: Jossey-Bass, 1975.

___. Higher Education: Who Pays? New York: McGraw-Hill, 1973.

Carnoy, Martin. Schooling in a Corporate Society. New York: David McKay, 1975.

Cheit, Earl. The New Depression in Higher Education. New York: Carnegie Commission on Education, 1975.

Congressional Quarterly. Education for a Nation. Washington, D.C.: Congressional Quarterly, annual.

Coons, John, et al. Private Wealth and Public Education. Cambridge: Harvard University Press, 1973.

Fein, Leonard. The Ecology of Public Schools. Indianapolis: Pegasus, 1971.

Gladieux, Lawrence. Congress and the Colleges. Lexington, Mass.: D.C. Heath, 1976.

Glazer, Nathan. Affirmative Discrimination. New York: Basic Books, 1975.

Katz, Michael. The Irony of Early School Reform. Cambridge: Harvard University Press, 1967.

___. Education Reform. Boston: Little, Brown, 1971.

Kirst, Michael. State, Schools, and Politics. Lexington, Mass.: D. C. Heath, 1972.

Jencks, Christopher. Inequality. New York: Basic Books, 1972.

Litt, Edgar. The Public Vocational University. New York: Holt, 1969.

Moynihan, Daniel P. Coping: On the Practice of Government. New York: Random House, 1973.

National Center for Education Statistics. The Condition of Education. Washington, D. C.: US Government Printing Office, annual.

New York State Education Department. Education Beyond High School. Albany, 1972.

Riesman, David, and Christopher Jencks. The Academic Revolution. Doubleday, 1968.

Rodgers, David. 110 Livingston Street. New York: Random House, 1968.

Sindler, Allan. Policy and Politics in America. Boston: Little, Brown, 1973.

___. Bakke, Defunis, and Minority Admissions. New York: Longman, 1978.

Spring, Joel. The Sorting Machine: National Education Policy since 1945. New York: David McKay, 1976.

Thomas, Norman. Education in National Politics. New York: David McKay, 1975.

Wirt, Frederick. Political Science and School Politics. Lexington, Mass.: D. C. Heath, 1976.

ABOUT THE AUTHORS

EDGAR LITT, Professor of Political Science, University of Connecticut, is the author of Ethnic Politics in America: The Public Vocational University, and other books and articles. He has also studied education policies as a Senior National Humanities Fellow in Britain and as a Fulbright Fellow in West Germany.

MICHAEL PARKINSON is lecturer in Political Theory and Institutions at the University of Liverpool. He has been Visiting Associate Professor in Political Science at Washington University in St. Louis from 1976 to the present.

Mr. Parkinson has published several pieces on the politics of education, and his articles and reviews have appeared in Political Studies, Parliamentary Affairs, and Town Planning.

Mr. Parkinson holds a B. A. from the University of Liverpool and an M. A. in Economics from the University of Manchester.